Expansive Civility

Expansive Civility

The American Chesterfield

by Lord Philip Dormer Stanhope, Earl of Chesterfield

Volume 2 in the Westphalia Press Civility Series

WESTPHALIA PRESS
An imprint of Policy Studies Organization

Westphalia Press
An imprint of Policy Studies Organization
1527 New Hampshire Ave., NW
Washington, D.C. 20036
dgutierrezs@ipsonet.org

ISBN-13: 978-1935907756
ISBN-10: 1935907751

Cover design by Taillefer Long at Illuminated Stories:
www.illuminatedstories.com

Updated material and comments on this edition
can be found at the Westphalia Press website:
www.westphaliapress.org

In Search of Civility

An archaic meaning of civility was 'study of the humanities,' and as a word it appears in the sixteenth century. The years have not blunted its importance; it is one of the guiding principles of *Wikipedia*, which informs readers that, "The civility policy is a standard of conduct that sets out how *Wikipedia* editors should interact. Stated simply, editors should always treat each other with consideration and respect. In order to keep the focus on improving the encyclopedia and to help maintain a pleasant editing environment, editors should behave politely, calmly and reasonably, even during heated debates."

Other voices also have been raised about the need to consider civility as a priority in an increasingly abrasive modern society. The Institute for Civility in Government in Houston, ably led by Cassandra Dahnke and Tomas Spath, has for many years hosted Washington seminars and blogs on the subject. Profesor J.M. Forni at Johns Hopkins has made a life's work out of studying the ramifications of civility. In the Hopkins alumni magazine he sums the current situation up when he writes:

E

We do have our manners. What we have lost are the manners of past generations. That we have manners, however, does not mean we ought to be perfectly happy with the manners we have. In fact, many Americans think that civility and manners are in decline, that this decline has increased in the past several years, and that there is a causal connection between incivility and violence. Does reality match the perception of a decline? Yes and no. There is little doubt that we are losing established forms of deference and respect. On the other hand, new forms of respect take the place of those becoming obsolete. A pregnant woman may not easily find a youngster willing to give her his seat on a bus. But the number of men willing to treat the same woman as an intellectual peer on the job is higher today than it was yesterday.

This does not mean that we should ignore the coarsening of social interaction that we have been witnessing in recent years. Our manners inevitably suffer when:
1. We are poorly trained in self-restraint.
2. We are used to seeing others as means to the satisfaction of our desires rather than ends in themselves.
3. We are overly concerned about financial gain and professional achievement.
4. We are constantly besieged by stress and fatigue.
5. We are surrounded by strangers who will remain strangers.
When some or all of these factors are at work, it becomes difficult to be considerate — and consideration is the ethical requirement of manners that are really good.

Clearly we need more people to take an interest in the topic rather than less. The Westphalia Press Civility Series demonstrates that the topic has many aspects, including etiquette and diplomacy. My friend Ambassador Mark Hambley suggests that there even might be some connection between the decline of cursive writing and the decline of civility. Unfortunately the current lack of civility in Washington is as noticeable or more noticeable than the state of the nation's handwriting. While politics has always been a competitive sport, common consensus is that the political life in the capital recently has become far more contentious than in recent memory.

F

The Westphalia Press Civility Series presents manners, etiquette, diplomacy, decent behavior, and politeness as fruit in the same orchard. The books are intended to be an accessible resource for studying facets of a subject that we think contributes to the current policy anxiety that has paralyzed decision making.

The subject has a universal aspect. Although we relish including George Washington as author of one of the titles in the collection, he actually found many of the maxims in his *Rules of Civility* in the literature of French Jesuits of the 1590s that was rendered in English by Francis Hawkins in London in 1640. By all account he was a man of manners no matter what the circumstances, and so we respectfully dedicate this series to his memory, in hopes that present day leaders will reflect on his example.

Paul Rich
President, Policy Studies Organization
Garfield House, Washington, D.C.

H

Eye nature's walks, shoot folly as it flies,
And catch the manners living as they rise.

J

THE
AMERICAN
CHESTERFIELD,
OR
WAY TO WEALTH,
HONOUR AND DISTINCTION;

BEING SELECTIONS FROM THE

LETTERS OF LORD CHESTERFIELD
TO HIS SON,

AND

Extracts from other eminent Authors on the
subject of Politeness:

WITH

ALTERATIONS AND ADDITIONS

SUITED TO THE

YOUTH OF THE UNITED STATES.

By a Member of the Philadelphia Bar.

———»»»●◉●⟨⟨⟨«———

Two principles in human nature reign ;
Self-love, to urge, and Reason to restrain :—
Self-love, the spring of motion, acts the soul ;
Reason's comparing balance rules the whole.
Essay on Man.

———»»»●◉●⟨⟨⟨«———

PHILADELPHIA:
PUBLISHED BY JOHN GRIGG,
No. 9, North Fourth Street.

Clark & Raser, Printers.
1827.

CONTENTS.

THE
American Chesterfield.

—••••••◉●••••—

As all young men, on their first outset in life, are in want of some experienced and friendly hand to bring them forward, and teach them a knowledge of the world; I think I cannot do the rising generation a greater service, than by directing the young man's steps, and teaching him how to make his way among the crowd. I will suppose him already instructed in the principles of religion, and the necessity of moral virtues, (for without these he must be most unhappy) and shall point out, under distinct heads, the qualifications necessary to make him well received in the world; without which, he cannot expect to bear his part in life, agreeably to his own wishes, or the duty he owes to society: and, as Modesty is the basis of a proper reception, I shall begin with that.

———

MODESTY.

MODESTY is a polite accomplishment, and generally an attendant upon merit. It is en-

gaging, to the highest degree, and wins the
hearts of all with whom we are acquainted. On
the contrary, none are more disgusting, in
company, than the impudent and presuming.

Those who mistake genuine modesty, which
is easily done, are apt to encourage in themselves a bashful timidity; or, at length aban-
doning that, to become pert and impudent. To
prevent this, I would have you consider, that
true modesty is the reflection of an honourable
mind, constantly impressed with a sense of
propriety; and always shows itself in avoiding
what might occasion merited censure. For
this reason, a modest man is as much so when
he is alone, as in company; and as subject to
blush in his closet, as when the eyes of multitudes are upon him.

This kind of modesty, although opposed to
impudence, is perfectly consistent with a proper assurance. One who is under its influence,
may, notwithstanding, perfectly possess himself; and say and do indifferent things, without any uneasiness or emotion. This open and
assured behaviour, is the natural consequence
of a knowledge of the world; and, above all,
of a fixed determination to do nothing inconsistent with decency and honour.

Every man ought to cherish and encourage,
in himself, this modest assurance. A man
without it, is liable to be made uneasy, by the
folly, impudence, or ill nature, of every person with whom he converses; and is lost to
every sense of honour. You may be modest,
and, at the same time, if you will, assured ; as
it is possible for the same person to be both
impudent and bashful. We have frequent instances of this latter odd kind of mixture, in

people of depraved minds and mean education; who, though they are not able to meet a man's eyes, or pronounce a sentence without confusion, can voluntarily commit the greatest villanies, or most indecent actions. Such persons seem to have made a resolution, to do evil, in spite of themselves, and in defiance of all those restraints which have been thrown in the way, by their natural tempers and inclinations.

There are no greater outlaws against good breeding than those who voluntarily throw off the restraints of modesty; and, conscious of impudence, profess it, with an air of humour; thinking to carry off one of the most inexcusable faults, by saying, with a gay tone, " I put an impudent face upon the matter." No man should be allowed the advantages of impudence, who knows he is impudent. If he knows it, he may as well be otherwise; and he ought to blush, when he sees he makes another redden; for nothing can atone for the want of modesty; without which, beauty is ungraceful, and wit detestable.

But, while I recommend modesty to your earnest attention, you are not to forget, that there is a false modesty, which is more pernicious than impudence itself. One who possesses it, has not the fortitude to resist the will or wish of another, although he secretly disapprove it. He acts to gratify others, rather than himself; and is frequently betrayed into the most abandoned practices, without a single act of his own will.—Study to guard against this unmanly disposition, more destructive of peace, virtue, and honour, than the greatest vice.

As nothing is more amiable, than true mo. desty, so nothing is more contemptible than false. The former makes a man ashamed to do any thing that is repugnant to the rules of reason; the latter makes him ashamed to do any thing that is opposite to the humour of his company: not only so, but it often restrains him from doing what is just and laudable. How despicable must you appear, in the eyes of all men of worth, and even in your own, if you give way to this ridiculous habit! Instead of that firmness, which commands respect, you must descend to that cringing manner, which every one may find convenient, but no one can treat in any other way, than with contempt.

Under the notion of modesty, you must not indulge yourself in a spiritless sheepishness. In this way, many have been lost to themselves, their families, their friends, and their country. When a man has taken care to pretend to nothing, but what he can justly aim at, and can, without injustice to any other, execute as well as others, it is even want of breeding or courage to be brow-beaten or elbowed out of his honest ambition. Modesty must be an act of the will; and, if a man, after having fixed on any thing laudable, from an unmanly bashfulness, shrinks away, he ought not to be angry that another succeeds, and that the world approves.

Modesty widely differs from an awkward bashfulness, which is as much to be condemned, as the other is to be applauded. To appear simple, is as ill-bred, as to be impudent. A young man ought to be able to come into a room, and address the company, without the least embarrassment.

A gentleman who is acquainted with life, enters a room with gracefulness and a modest assurance, addresses even persons he does not know, in an easy and natural manner, and without the least embarrassment. This is the characteristic of good breeding, a very necessary knowledge in our intercourse with men; for one of inferior parts, with the behaviour of a gentleman, is frequently better received than a man of sense, with the address and manners of a clown.

Ignorance and vice are the only things of which we need be ashamed. Avoid these, and you may go into any company you will: not that I would have a young man throw off all dread of appearing abroad, as a fear of offending or being disesteemed, will make him preserve a proper decorum. Some persons, from experiencing the inconveniences of false modesty, have run into the other extreme, and acquired the character of impudent. This is as great a fault as the other. A well bred man keeps himself within the two, and steers the middle way. He is easy and firm in every company; is modest, but not bashful; steady, but not impudent. He copies the manners of the better people, and conforms to their customs with ease and attention.

Until we can present ourselves, in all companies, with coolness and unconcern, we can never present ourselves well; nor will a man ever be supposed to have kept good company, or ever be acceptable in such company, if he cannot appear there easy and unembarrassed. A modest assurance, in every part of life, is the most advantageous qualification we can possibly acquire.

The man who is ignorant of his own merit, is no less a fool, than he who is constantly displaying it. A man of understanding avails himself of his abilities, but never boasts of them; whereas, the timid and bashful can never push himself in life, but will be always kept behind, by the forward and bustling. Instead of becoming insolent, a man of sense, under a consciousness of merit, is more modest. He behaves himself with firmness, but without the least presumption. Thus manners are every thing: what is impudence, in one, is proper assurance, only, in another; for firmness is commendable, but an overbearing conduct is disgusting.

Forwardness being the very reverse of modesty, follow, rather than lead, the company: that is, join in discourse upon subjects, rather than start one of your own. If you have talents, you will have opportunities enough of showing them, on every topic of conversation; and if you have none, it is better to expose yourself upon a subject of other people's, than one of your own.

But, be particularly careful not to speak of yourself, if you can help it. An impudent fellow intrudes himself, abruptly, upon all occasions, and is ever the hero of his own story. Others will colour their arrogance with "It may seem strange, indeed, that I should talk in this manner, of myself; it is what I by no means like, and should never do, if I had not been cruelly and unjustly accused: but, when my character is attacked, it is a justice I owe to myself, to defend it." This veil is too thin, not to be seen through, on the first inspection.

Others, again, with more art, will *modestly*

boast of all the principal virtues, by calling these virtues weaknesses, and saying they are so unfortunate as to fall into weaknesses. " I cannot see persons suffer," says one of this cast, " without relieving them; though my circumstances are very unable to afford it.—I cannot avoid speaking truth, though it is often very imprudent," and so on.

This angling for praise, is so prevailing a principle, that it frequently stoops to the lowest objects. Men will often boast of doing that, which, if true, would be rather a disgrace to them, than otherwise. One man affirms that he rode twenty miles, within the hour: it is probably a lie; but, suppose he did, what then? He had a good horse under him, and is a good jockey. Another swears he has often, at a sitting, drank five or six bottles, to his own share. Out of respect to him, I will believe him a liar, for I would not wish to think him a beast.

These, and many more, are the follies of idle people; which, while they think they procure them esteem, in reality make them despised.

To avoid this contempt, therefore, never speak of yourself, at all, unless necessity obliges you; and, even then, take care to do it in such a manner, that it may not be construed into fishing for applause. Whatever perfections you may have, be assured, people will find them out; but, whether they do or not, nobody will take them upon your own word. The less you say of yourself, the more the world will give you credit for; and the more you say, the less they will believe you.

As a further inducement to the acquisition of

modesty, let me assure you, that it recommends every talent that you would wish to possess. It heightens all the virtues that it accompanies; like the shades in painting, it raises and rounds every figure, and makes the colours more beautiful, though not so glaring as they would be without it.

Modesty is not only an ornament, but also a guard, to virtue. It is a kind of quick and delicate feeling in the soul, which makes her shrink and withdraw herself from every thing in which there is danger. Nothing can tend more to damp this amiable sensibility, than that kind of conduct, which seems indirectly to recommend a total disregard to it, as the perfection of breeding, which keeps a man in countenance, not because he is innocent, but because he is shameless.

VANITY.

I now come to a point, of much less, but yet of very great consequence, at your first setting out. Be extremely upon your guard against VANITY, the common failing of inexperienced youth; but particularly against that kind of vanity, that dubs a man a coxcomb,—a character which once acquired, is indelible. It is not to be imagined, by how many different ways, vanity defeats its own purpose. One man decides peremptorily, upon every subject, betrays his ignorance upon many, and shows a disgusting presumption upon the rest. Another desires to appear successful among the women: he hints at the encouragement he has received, from those of the most distinguished rank and beauty; and intimates a particular connexion with some one. If it is true, it is ungenerous; if false, it is infamous: but, in either case, he destroys the reputation which he wishes to acquire. Some flatter their vanity, by little extraneous objects, which have not the least relation to themselves—such as being descended from, related to, or acquainted with people of eminent characters and distinguished merit. They talk perpetually of their grandfather such-a-one, their uncle such-a-one, and their intimate friend, Mr. such-a-one, with whom, possibly, they are hardly acquainted. But, admitting it all to be as they would have it; what then? Have they the more merit for these accidents? Certainly not. On the contrary, their taking up adventitious things, proves their want of intrinsic merit—a rich man never borrows. Take this rule for granted, as never failing, that you must never seem to affect the character in which you have a mind to shine. Modesty is the virtue which secures merited applause. The affectation of courage, will make even a brave man pass only for a bully; as the affectation of wit will make a man of parts pass for a coxcomb. By this modesty, I do not mean timidity, and awkward bashfulness. On the contrary, be inwardly firm and steady, know your own value, whatever it may be, and act upon that principle; but take care to let nobody discover that you do know your own value. Whatever real merit you have, other people will discover; and people always magnify their own discoveries, as they lessen those of others.

If you wish to aspire to an exalted character, remember, there is nothing more baneful to it, than a display of vanity. It always betokens a littleness of soul. The vain man betrays his own consciousness of a want of inherent worth, by valuing himself upon things which can neither evince worth, nor confer it. He estimates his horse, in proportion to his youth, strength and beauty, not his trappings; yet he measures his own claims to respectability, not by the goodness of his heart, or the endowments of his mind, but by a fine suit of clothes, a magnificent house, splendid apartments, a bauble, a snuff-box, or a gold-headed cane. As soon as a man of this description is discovered, he loses respect. We cannot entertain an exalted opinion of a person, who has so mean an opinion of himself. If he prefers trifles to himself, we cannot be accused of injustice, should the same preference be adopted by us.

To be cured of this folly, you have only to witness when you see a person behave in this manner, what passes within yourself. When, with all his vapouring pretensions to greatness, he imagines himself rousing your admiration, and securing your respect, does he not excite your contempt? You may take it for granted, were you to imitate his example, he would feel exactly as you now do. If you wish to secure admiration, endeavour to obtain it by excellence; which has this advantage, that it not only attracts the respect of the valuable part of mankind, but retains it. Vanity has its gratifications, but they are momentary; and the misfortune is, the vain are much more likely to be tormented by neglect, than delighted with flattery and attention.

LYING.

Of all the vices, there is none more criminal, more mean, and more ridiculous, than LYING. The end designed by it, is very seldom accomplished; for lies are always discovered, at one time or another; and yet there are persons who indulge in this vice, who are otherwise of good principles, and have not received a bad education.

Lies generally proceed from vanity, cowardice, and a revengeful disposition, and sometimes from a mistaken notion of self-defence.

Some, unfortunately, through early habits, have acquired such a propensity to lying, that they cannot avoid it, even when it answers no purpose; nor can scarcely speak the truth, when it is their interest. Others who do not indulge in gross lies, are much addicted to what may be termed *refined* lying. They represent the outlines of a fact, but give to it a colouring, calculated to leave a wrong impression. This is a mode of lying more pernicious than the other, and equally disgraceful; and both are equally beneath any man who has the slightest claim to honour.

But there is a kind of lies, which not only stamps the character with disgrace, but fixes upon it a charge of cruelty;—I mean the malicious lie, told expressly to injure, and without any motive arising from necessity or self-love.

He who tells a malicious lie, with a view of injuring the person of whom he speaks, may gratify his wish, for a while, but will, in the end, find it recoil upon himself. As soon as he is detected (and detected he most certainly will be) he is despised, for the infamous attempt; and whatever he may say, hereafter, of that person, will be considered as false, whether it be so or not.

If a man lies, shuffles, or equivocates, (for, in fact, they are all alike) by way of excuse for any thing he has said or done, he aggravates, rather than lessens the offence. The person to whom the lie is told, has a right to know the truth, or there would have been no occasion to have framed a falsehood. This person, of course, will think himself ill treated, for being a second time affronted; for what can be a greater affront than an attempt to impose upon any man's understanding? Besides, lying, in excuse for a fault, betrays fear; than which nothing is more dastardly, and unbecoming the character of a gentleman.

There is nothing more manly, or more noble, if we have done wrong, than frankly to own it. It is the only way of meeting forgiveness. Indeed, confessing a fault, and asking pardon, with great minds, is considered as a sufficient atonement. "I have been betrayed into an error," or, "I have injured you, Sir, and am heartily ashamed of it, and sorry for it," has frequently disarmed the person injured; and, where he would have been our enemy, has made him our friend.

There are persons, also, whose *vanity* leads them to tell a thousand lies. They persuade themselves, that, if it be no way injurious to others, it is harmless and innocent; and they shelter their falsehoods under the softer name of untruths. These persons are foolish enough to imagine, that if they can recite any thing wonderful, they draw the attention of the company; and if they themselves are the objects of that wonder, they are looked up to as extraordinary persons. This has made many a man see things, that never were in being, hear things that never were said, and achieve feats that never were attempted; dealing always in the marvellous. Such may be assured, however unwilling the persons with whom they are conversing, may be to laugh in their faces, that they hold them, secretly, in the highest contempt; for he who will tell a lie thus idly, will not scruple to tell a greater, where his interest is concerned.

There is another sort of lies, inoffensive enough in themselves, but wonderfully ridiculous: I mean those lies suggested by a mistaken vanity, that defeat the very end for which they are calculated, and terminate in the humiliation and confusion of their author, who is sure to be detected. These are chiefly narrative and historical lies, all intended to do infinite honour to their author. He is always the hero of his own romances; he has been in dangers, from which nobody but himself ever escaped; he has seen with his own eyes whatever other people have heard or read of: he has had more *bonnes fortunes** than ever he knew women; and has ridden more miles post, in one day, than ever courier went in two. He is soon discovered, and as soon becomes the object of universal contempt and ridicule.

The prudence and necessity of often concealing the truth, insensibly seduces people to violate it. It is the only art of mean capaci-

---

* Happy chances—fortunate meetings.

ties, and the only refuge of mean spirits. Whereas, concealing the truth upon proper occasions, is as prudent and innocent, as telling a lie upon any occasion, is infamous and foolish.

But there is a species of lying, of which I must advertise you, the more pernicious, as it is the more common; I mean *party-lying*. I have often wondered to see men of probity, who would scorn to utter a falsehood for their own particular advantage, so readily countenance a lie, when it is become the voice of their faction. How are we to account for it, that men of honour, in their own concerns, should become notorious liars in their party? Is it possible, they can think that a lie is dissipated by the multitude of those who partake in it? And that, though the weight of a falsehood is too heavy for the reputation of one, it grows light when shared among many? It is true, though multitudes, who join in a lie, cannot exempt them from the guilt, it may screen them from the shame of it; and this, with men of not very delicate minds, may be sufficient to confirm them in the practice. The lie does good at least to their party. But, whatever may be the motive, still it is lying; a shameful practice, to be discarded from every honourable mind. It is the most likely, however, to seduce even the lover of truth, and for that reason, requires to be the more vigorously guarded against.

Remember, that, though truth be sometimes troublesome, it is always honourable. It has this advantage, too, it needs nothing to help it out. It is always at hand, sits upon our lips, and is ready to drop out before we are aware; whereas a lie is troublesome, it sets a man's invention on the rack, and one lie needs a great many more, to make it good. It is like building on a false foundation, which constantly stands in need of props, to keep it up, and proves, at last, more chargeable, than to have raised a substantial building, at first, upon a solid foundation. Add to this, the liar is the last man to know that he is found out; and is in deep disgrace for years before he is aware.

ENVY.

Now that we are upon the subject of the creeping vices, let me caution you against Envy; which consists in feeling pained at the prosperity of another. This unhappy disposition, if you encourage it, will do more to degrade you, and render you wretched, than all the other passions and vices together. The envious man is in pain upon all occasions that ought to give him pleasure. The relish of his life is inverted; and the objects which administer the highest satisfaction, to those who are exempt from this passion, give the sharpest pangs to persons who are subject to it. All the perfections of their fellow creatures are odious:—youth, beauty, valour, and wisdom, are provocations of their displeasure.

The condition of the envious man, cannot but be emphatically miserable. He is not only incapable of rejoicing in another's merit or success, but lives in a world where all mankind are in a plot against his quiet, by studying their own happiness. Their reliefs show their torments. They do not aim at rivalling the envied person, by honourable exertions, but cast dust in the eyes of their competitor, or trip up his heels in the race, and feast, with a rancorous rapture, on those blemishes, which the excellence that they envy, renders the more perceivable.

Low minds are almost always the prey of this hateful passion; and to live above it, is the strongest evidence of an exalted understanding. The mind that is conscious of its want of intrinsic merit, will be ever on the rack at the display of it in others; and will be sure to feel torment, on perceiving others in possession of any thing, on which it sets a high value, but which it does not possess.

Low people, in good circumstances, with fine clothes, and equipages, will insolently show contempt for all those who cannot afford as fine clothes, as good equipage, and who have not (as their term is) as much money in their pockets. On the other hand, they are gnawed with envy, and cannot help discovering it, at those who surpass them in any of these articles; which are far from being sure criterions of merit. They are, likewise, jealous of being slighted; and consequently suspicious and captious: they are eager and hot about trifles; because trifles were, at first, their affairs of moment.

In a word, envy is certainly one of the meanest and most tormenting of all passions; since there is hardly any body that has not something for an envious man to envy; so that he can never be happy, while he sees any body else so.

Should you indulge this ignoble passion, you

may bid adieu to all excellence; since it is its nature, to waste that energy in secret sufferance, which might have contributed to raise the character, had it been cherished by a generous disposition.

———

GOOD BREEDING.

WITHOUT GOOD BREEDING, every other qualification will be imperfect, unadorned, and, to a certain degree, unavailing.

Good breeding being the result of good sense and good nature, it is not wonderful, that people deficient in the one, should not be possessed of the others. The modes of it varying according to persons, places, and circumstances, cannot indeed be acquired, otherwise than by time and observation; but the substance is every where and always the same.

What good morals are to society in general, good manners are to particular societies, their bond and security. Of all actions, next to that of performing a good one, the consciousness of rendering a civility, is the most grateful.

As learning, honour, and virtue, are absolutely necessary, to gain you the esteem of mankind, politeness and good breeding are equally necessary, to make you welcome and agreeable, in conversation and common life. Great talents, such as eloquence, the ability of a statesman, and a genius for the acquirement of the philosophical sciences, are above the generality of the world; who neither possess them themselves, nor judge of them rightly in others: but all people are judges of the lesser talents, such as civility, affability, and an obliging, agreeable address and manner; because they feel their effects, as making society easy and pleasing. Good sense must, in many cases, determine good breeding; because the same thing that would be civil at one time, and to one person, would be quite otherwise at another time, and to another person. But there are some general rules of good breeding, that hold true at all times, and in all cases. As, for example, it is always extremely rude to answer only Yes or No, to any body, without adding Sir, or Madam, according to the quality of the person to whom you speak. It is likewise extremely rude, not to give proper attention, and a civil answer, when people speak to you; or to go away, or be doing something else; for that convinces them that you despise them, and do not think it worth your while to hear or answer what they say. I need not tell you how rude it is to take the best place in the room; or to seize immediately upon what you like at table, without offering first to help others, as if you considered nobody but yourself. On the contrary, you should always endeavour to procure all the conveniences you can, to the people you are with. Besides, being civil, which is absolutely necessary, the perfection of good breeding is, to be civil with ease, and in a gentleman-like manner. For this, you should observe those people, who excel in it, and whose politeness seems as easy and natural, as any other part of their conversation. But, pray, remember never to be ashamed of doing what is right. You would have a great deal of reason to be ashamed, if you were not civil; but what reason can you have to be ashamed of being civil; and why not say a civil and an obliging thing, as easily and as naturally as you would ask what o'clock it is? This kind of bashfulness, which is justly called, by the French, *mauvaise honte*,* is the distinguishing characteristic of a booby, who is frightened out of his wits, when people of fashion speak to him; and, when he is to answer them, blushes, stammers, can hardly get out what he would say, and becomes really ridiculous, from a groundless fear of being laughed at; whereas, a really well-bred man would speak, to all the great men in the world, with as little concern, and as much ease, as he would speak to you.

These, some will say, are little things. It is true, they are little; but it is as true, too, that they are necessary things. As they are mere matters of usage and mode, it is no disgrace for any one of your age to be ignorant of them; and the most compendious way of learning them, is, fairly to avow your ignorance, and to consult those, who, from long usage and experience, know them best. Good sense, and good nature, suggest civility in general; but, in good breeding, there are a thousand little delicacies, which are established only by custom; and it is these little elegancies of manners which distinguish a courtier, and a man of fashion, from the vulgar. The best bred people will always be the best received, wherever they go. Good manners are the settled medium of social, as *specie* is of commercial, life: returns are equally expected for both; and people will no more advance

---

* Ill-timed shame—excessive bashfulness.

their civility to a bear, than their money to a bankrupt.

We are all so formed, that our understandings are generally the dupes of our hearts; that is, of our passions; and the surest way to the former is through the latter; which must be engaged by the *leniores virtutes** alone, and the manner of exerting them. The insolent civility of a proud man, is (for example) if possible, more shocking than his rudeness could be; because he shows you, by his manner, that he thinks it mere condescension in him; and that his goodness alone bestows upon you what you have no pretence to claim. He intimates his protection, instead of his friendship, by a gracious nod, instead of an usual bow; and signifies rather his consent that you may, than his invitation that you should sit or walk, eat or drink, with him.

The reluctant liberality of a purse-proud man, insults the distresses which it sometimes relieves. He takes care to make you feel your own misfortunes, and the difference between your situation and his; both which he insinuates to be justly merited: yours, by your folly; his, by his wisdom. The arrogant pedant does not communicate, but promulgates his knowledge. He does not give it *to* you, but he inflicts it *upon* you; and is (if possible) more desirous to show you your own ignorance, than his own learning. Such manners as these, not only in the particular instances which I have mentioned, but likewise in all others, shock that little pride and vanity, which every man has in his heart; and oblite-

---

* Milder virtues.

rate in us the obligation for the favour conferred, by reminding us of the motive which produced, and the manner which accompanied it.

There can be no objection to this breeding which I recommend, from any great difficulty in its attainment. We seldom see a person, let him be ever so ill bred, wanting in respect to those whom he acknowledges to be his superiors: all that I contend for, then, is the manner of showing it. The well-bred man expresses it naturally and easily; while he who is unused to good company, expresses it awkwardly. Study, then, to show that respect which every one wishes to show in an easy and graceful way. And let me assure you, that I owe much more of the success which I have had in the world, to my manners, than to any superior degree of merit or knowledge. I desired to please, and I neglected none of the means. This, I can assure you, without any false modesty, is the truth.

Yet, to be well-bred, without ceremony; easy, without negligence; steady and intrepid, with modesty; genteel, without affectation; insinuating, without meanness; cheerful, without being noisy; frank, without indiscretion, and secret, without mysteriousness; to know the proper time and place for whatever you say or do, and to do it with an air of condition: all this is not so soon or so easily learned, as people imagine; but requires observation and time. The world is an immense folio, which demands a great deal of time and attention, to be read and understood as it ought to be.

As to this good breeding, a friend of yours and mine has very justly defined it to be, the

result of much good sense, some good nature,
and a little self-denial for the sake of others,
and with a view to obtain the same indulgence
from them. Taking this for granted (as I
think it cannot be disputed) it is astonishing,
that any body, who has good sense and good
nature, can essentially fail in good breeding.
As to the modes of it, indeed, they vary, according to persons, places, and circumstances;
and are to be acquired only by observation and
experience; but the substance of it is every
where and eternally the same. Good manners, as I have already observed, are, to particular societies, what good morals are to society in general: their security and their ce-
ment; and, as laws are enacted to enforce good
morals, or at least to prevent the ill effects of
bad, so there are certain rules of civility, universally implied and received, to enforce good
manners, and punish bad. Indeed, there seems
to me to be less difference, both between the
crimes and punishments, than at first one
would imagine. The immoral man, who invades another's property, is justly hanged for
it; and the ill-bred man, who by his ill manners invades and disturbs the quiet and comforts of private life, is, by common consent, as
justly banished from society. Mutual complaisance, attention, and sacrifices of little conveniences, are as natural an implied compact
between civilized people, as protection and
obedience are between kings and subjects:
whoever, in either case, violates that compact,
justly forfeits all advantages arising from it.
For my own part, I really think, that, next to
the consciousness of doing a good action, that
of doing a civil one is the most pleasing: and

the epithet which I should covet the most,
next to that of Aristides, would be that of
well-bred. Thus much for good breeding in
general. I will now consider some of its various incidents and modes.

Solid knowledge, as I have often told you,
is the first and great foundation of your future
fortune and character; for I never mention to
you the two much greater points of religion
and morality, because I cannot possibly suspect you, as to either of them. But, remember, that manners must adorn knowledge, and
smooth its way through the world. Like a
great, rough diamond, it may do very well in
a closet, by way of curiosity, and also for its
intrinsic value; but it will never be worn, nor
shine, if it is not polished. Be convinced, that
there are no persons, so insignificant and in-
considerable, that may not, some time or other,
and in some thing or other, have it in their
power to be of use to you; which they certainly will not, if you have once shown them
contempt. Wrongs are often forgiven, but
contempt never is. Our pride remembers it,
for ever. It implies a discovery of weaknesses,
which we are much more careful to conceal
than crimes. Many a man will confess his
crimes, to a common friend; but I never knew
a man who would tell his silly weaknesses to
his most intimate one: as many a friend will
tell us our faults, without reserve, who will
not so much as hint at our follies. The latter
discovery is too mortifying to our self-love,
either to tell to another, or to be told of one's
self.

Next to manners, are exterior graces of
person and address; which adorn manners, as

manners adorn knowledge. To say that they please, engage, and charm, as they most indisputably do, is saying, that one should do every thing possible to acquire them. The graceful manner of speaking is, particularly, what I shall always hollow in your ears, as Hotspur hollowed *Mortimer* to Henry IV.; and like him, too, I have a mind to have a starling taught to say, *speak distinctly and gracefully.*

In order to judge of the inside of others, study your own. Men, in general, are very much alike; and though one man has one prevailing passion, and another has another, yet their operations are much the same; and whatever engages or disgusts, pleases or offends you, in others, will, *mutatis mutandis,** engage, disgust, please, or offend others, in you. Observe, with the utmost attention, all the operations of your own mind, the nature of your passions, and the various motives that determine your will; and you may, in a great degree, know all mankind. For instance; do you find yourself hurt and mortified, when another makes you feel his superiority, and your own inferiority, in knowledge, parts, rank, or fortune? You will certainly take great care not to make a person, whose good will, good word, interest, esteem, or friendship, you would gain, feel that superiority in you, in case you have it. If disagreeable insinuations, sly sneers, or repeated contradictions, teaze and irritate you, would you use them, where you wished to engage and please? Surely not; and I hope you wish to engage and please, almost universally. The temptation of saying a

---

* Changing what ought to be changed.

smart or witty thing, or *bon mot*, and the malicious applause with which it is commonly received, has made people who can say them, and still oftener people who think they can, but cannot, and yet try, more enemies, and implacable ones, too, than any one thing that I know of. When such things, then, shall happen to be said, at your expense, (as sometimes they certainly will) reflect seriously upon the sentiments of uneasiness, anger, and resentment, which they excite in you; and consider whether it can be prudent, by the same means, to excite the same sentiments in others, against you. It is a decided folly, to lose a friend, for a jest; but, in my mind, it is not a much less degree of folly, to make an enemy of an indifferent, and neutral person, for the sake of a *bon mot*. When things of this kind happen to be said of you, the most prudent way is to seem not to suppose that they are meant at you; but to avoid showing whatever degree of anger you may feel inwardly; and, should they be so plain, that you cannot be supposed ignorant of their meaning, to join in the laugh of the company, against yourself; acknowledge the hit to be a fair one, and the jest a good one, and play off the whole thing, in seeming good humour: but by no means reply in the same way; which only shows that you are hurt, and publishes the victory which you might have concealed.

In promiscuous companies, you should vary your address, agreeably to the different ages of the persons to whom you speak: it would be rude and absurd to talk of your courtships or your pleasures to men of certain dignity and gravity, to clergymen, or men in years;

B

but still you should be as easy with them, as
with others; your manner only should be va-
ried; you should, if possible, double your respect and attention to them: and were you to
insinuate occasionally, that, from their observation and experience, you wish to profit, you
would insensibly win their esteem; for flattery, if not fulsome and gross, is agreeable to
all.

In these companies, you must not be discouraged, and think yourself either slighted or
laughed at, because you see others, older and
more used to the world, easier, more familiar,
and consequently rather better received in
those companies, than yourself. In time, your
turn will come; and, if you do but show an inclination, a desire to please, though you should
be embarrassed, or even err in the means
(which must necessarily happen to you at first)
yet the will (to use a vulgar expression) will
be taken for the deed; and people, instead of
laughing at you, will be glad to instruct you.
Good sense can give you only the great outlines of good breeding: nothing but observation and usage can give you the delicate
touches, and the fine colouring. You will naturally endeavour to show the utmost respect
to people of certain ranks and characters, and
consequently you will show it; but the proper,
the delicate manner of showing that respect,
can be acquired only by time and observation.

Another thing, which I most earnestly recommend to you, in every part of the world
where you may happen to be, is not only real,
but seeming attention to whomsoever you
speak, or to whomsoever speaks to you. There
is nothing so brutally shocking, nor so little

forgiven, as a seeming inattention to the person who is speaking to you. I have known many a man knocked down, for (in my opinion) a much slighter provocation, than that shocking inattention which I mean. I have seen many people, who, while you are speaking to them, instead of looking at, and attending to you, fix their eyes upon the ceiling, or some other part of the room, look out of the window, play with a dog, twirl their snuff-box, or pick their nose. Nothing discovers a little, futile, frivolous mind, more than this, and nothing is so offensively ill-bred: it is an explicit declaration, on your part, that the most trifling object deserves your attention, more than all that can be said by the person who is speaking to you. Judge of the sentiments of hatred and resentment, which such treatment must excite, in every breast where there dwells any degree of self-love; and I am sure, I never yet met with that breast where there was not a great deal. I repeat it again and again, (for it is highly necessary that you remember it,) that that sort of vanity and self-love is inseparable from human nature, whatever may be its rank or condition; even your servant will sooner forget and forgive a beating, than any manifest mark of slight and contempt. Be, therefore, I beg of you, not only really, but seemingly and manifestly, attentive to whomsoever speaks to you; nay more, take their tone, and tune yourself to their unison. Be serious with the serious, and gay with the gay. In assuming these various shapes, endeavour to make each of them seem to sit easy upon you, and even to appear to be your own natural turn. This is the true and useful versatility, of which

which a thorough knowledge of the world at
once teaches the utility and the means of acquiring.

I am very sure, at least I hope, that you
will never make use of a silly expression,
which is the favourite expression, and the absurd excuse of all fools and blockheads; "*I
cannot do such a thing*," a thing by no means
either morally or physically impossible. "*I
cannot* attend long together to the same thing,"
says one fool: that is, he is such a fool that he
will not. It is a shame and an absurdity, for
any man to say, that he cannot do all those
things which are commonly done by all the
rest of mankind.

In mixed companies, with your equals, (for
in mixed companies all people are, to a certain degree, equal) greater ease and liberty
are allowed; but they too have their bounds
within *bienséance.** Their is a social respect
necessary: you may start your own subject of
conversation with modesty; taking great care.
however, *de ne jamais parler de cordes dans
la maison d'un pendû.*† Your words, gestures.
and attitudes, have a greater degree of latitude, though by no means an unbounded one.
You may have your hands in your pockets.
take snuff, sit, stand, or occasionally walk, as
you like: but I believe you would not think it
very *bienséant*‡ to whistle, put on your hat.
loosen your garters or your buckles, lie down

---

* Decency—decorum.

† Never to speak of ropes, in the house of
one who has been hung; never to distress the
afflicted.

‡ Decorous.

upon a couch, or go to bed and welter in an easy chair. These are negligences and freedoms which one can take only when quite alone: they are injurious to superiors, shocking and offensive to equals, brutal and insulting to inferiors. That easiness of carriage and behaviour, which is exceedingly engaging, widely differs from negligence and inattention, and by no means implies that one may do whatever one pleases: it only means that one is not to be stiff, formal, embarrassed, disconcerted, and ashamed, like country bumpkins, and people who have never been in good company; but it requires great attention to *les bienséances*, and a scrupulous observation of them: whatever one ought to do, is to be done with ease and unconcern; whatever is improper, must not be done at all. But example explains things best, and I will put a pretty strong case. Suppose you and me alone together; I believe you will allow that I have as good a right to unlimited freedom in your company, as either you or I can possibly have in any other; and I am apt to believe, too, that you would indulge me in that freedom as far as any body would. But, notwithstanding this, do you imagine that I should think there were no bounds to that freedom? I assure you, I should not think so; and I take myself to be as much tied down by a certain degree of good manners, to you, as by other degrees of them to other people. Were I to show you, by a manifest inattention to what you said to me, that I was thinking of something else, the whole time; were I to yawn extremely, or snore, in your company, I should think that I behaved myself to you like a beast, and should not expect that you would care to frequent me.—In mixed companies, also, different ages and sexes are to be differently addressed. Men of a certain age, gravity, and dignity, justly expect, from young people, a degree of deference and regard. You should be full as easy with them, as with people of your own years: but your manner must be different; more respect must be implied; and it is not amiss to insinuate, that from them you expect to learn. It flatters and comforts age, for not being able to take a part in the joy and titter of youth. To women, you should always address yourself with great respect and attention; their sex is entitled to it, and it is among the duties of *bienséance:* at the same time, that respect is very properly and very agreeably mixed with a degree of *enjouement,** if you have it.

Another important point of *les bienséances,* seldom enough attended to, is, not to run your own present humour and disposition indiscriminately against every body: but to observe and conform to theirs. For example: if you happened to be in high good humour, and a flow of spirits, would you go and sing a *pont neuf*† or cut a caper, to a la maréchale de Coigny, the Pope's nuncio, or the Abbé Sallier, or to any person of natural gravity and melancholy, or who at that time should be in grief? I believe not: as, on the other hand, I suppose, that if you were in low spirits, or real grief, you would not choose to bewail your situation with Madame Blot. If you cannot

* Gaiety.
† New Bridge: the name of a song, then fashionable at Paris.

command your present humour and disposition, single out those to converse with, who happen to be in a humour the nearest to your own.

Peremptoriness and decision, in young people, is *contraire aux bienséances:** they should seldom seem to assert, and always use some mitigating expression, which softens the manner, without giving up, or even weakening the thing. People of more age and experience expect, and are entitled to, that degree of deference.

Compose your countenance to an air of gentleness and *douceur;*† use some expressions of diffidence of your own opinion, and deference to other people's ; such as, If I might be permitted to say—Is it not rather so? At least, I have the greatest reason to be diffident of myself.—Such mitigating, engaging words, do by no means weaken your argument; but, on the contrary, make it more powerful, by making it more pleasing. If it be a quick and hasty manner of speaking, that people mistake for decided and peremptory, prevent their mistakes, for the future, by speaking more deliberately, and using a softer tone of voice: as, in this case, you are free from the guilt, be free also from the suspicion. Mankind, as I have often told you, are governed more by appearances, than by realities: and, with regard to opinion, one had better be really rough and hard, with the appearance of gentleness and softness, than just the reverse. Few people have penetration enough to discover, attention enough to observe, or even concern enough to exa-

---

* Contrary to decency.
† Softness, mildness.

mine, beyond the exterior; they take their notions from the surface, and go no deeper; they commend, as the gentlest and best natured man in the world, that man who has the most engaging exterior manner, though possibly they have been but once in his company. An air, a tone of voice, a composure of countenance to mildness and softness, which are all easily acquired, do the business; and, without further examination, and possibly with the contrary qualities, that man is reckoned the gentlest, the most modest, and the best natured man alive.

I must add another caution, which is, that, upon no account, whatever, you put your fingers, as too many people are apt to do, into your nose or ears. It is the most shocking, nasty, vulgar rudeness, that can be offered to company: it disgusts one, it turns one's stomach. Wash your ears well, every morning, and blow your nose in your handkerchief, whenever you have occasion: but, by the way, without looking at it afterwards. There should be, in the least, as well as in the greatest parts, of a gentlemen, *les manières nobles.** Sense will teach you some, observation others: attend carefully to the manners, the diction, the motions, of people of the first fashion, and form your own upon them. On the other hand, observe a little those of the vulgar, in order to avoid them: for, though the things which they say or do, may be the same, the manner is always totally different; and in that, and nothing else, consists the characteristic of a man of fashion. The lowest peasant speaks, moves,

---

* Dignified manners.

dresses, eats, and drinks, as much as a man of
the first fashion; but does them all quite differently; so that, by doing and saying most
things in a manner opposite to that of the vulgar, you have a great chance of doing and
saying them right. There are gradations in
awkwardness and vulgarism, as there are in
every thing else. But good breeding consists
in more than merely not being ill bred. To
return a bow, speak when you are spoken to,
and say nothing rude, are such negative acts
of good breeding, that they are little more
than not being a brute. Would it not be a
very poor commendation of any man's cleanliness, to say that he was not offensive? If we
wish for the good will and esteem of our acquaintance, our good breeding must be active,
cheerful, officious, and seducing.

For example, should you invite any one to
dine or sup with you, recollect whether ever
you had observed him to prefer one thing to
another, and endeavour to procure that thing:
when at table, say, " At such a time, I think
you seemed to give this dish a preference, I
therefore ordered it." " This is the wine I
observed you best like, I have therefore been
at some pains to procure it." Trifling as these
things may appear, they prove an attention
to the person to whom they are said; and, as
attention in trifles is the test of respect, the
compliment will not be lost.

I need only refer you to your own breast.
How have these little attentions, when shown
you by others, flattered that self-love from
which no man is free? They incline and attach us to that person, and prejudice us afterwards to all that he says or does. The decla-

rations of the women, in a great degree, stamp
a man's reputation, of being either ill or well
bred. You must then, in a manner, overwhelm
them with these attentions; they are used to
them, and naturally expect them, and to do
them justice, they are seldom lost upon them.
You must be sedulous to wait upon them,
pick up with alacrity any thing they drop, and
be very officious in procuring their carriages
or their chairs, in public places; be blind to
what you should not see, and deaf to what
you should not hear. Opportunities of showing these attentions are continually presenting
themselves; but, in case they should not, you
must study to create them.

It is good breeding, alone, that can prepossess people in your favour, at first sight; more
time being necessary to discover greater talents. This good breeding, you know, does
not consist in low bows and formal ceremony;
but in an easy, civil, and respectful behaviour.
You will therefore take care, to answer with
complaisance, when you are spoken to; to
place yourself at the lower end of the table,
unless bid to go higher; not to eat awkwardly
or dirtily; not to sit when others stand: and
to do all this with an air of complaisance, and
not with a grave, sour look, as if you did it all
unwillingly. I do not mean a silly, insipid
smile, that fools have when they would be
civil; but an air of sensible good humour. I
hardly know any thing so difficult to attain, or
so necessary to possess, as perfect good breeding; which is equally inconsistent with a stiff
formality, an impertinent forwardness, and an
awkward bashfulness. A little ceremony is
often necessary; a certain degree of firmness

is absolutely so; and an outward modesty is extremely becoming: the knowledge of the world, and your own observations, must, and alone can, tell you the proper quantities of each. It is the compound result of different things: a complaisance, a flexibility, but not a servility of manners: an air of softness in the countenance, gesture, and expression; equally, whether you concur or differ with the person you converse with. Observe those carefully who have that *douceur** which charms you and others; and your own good sense will soon enable you to discover the different ingredients of which it is composed. You must be more particularly attentive to this *douceur*, whenever you are obliged to refuse what is asked of you, or to say what in itself cannot be very agreeable to those to whom you say it. It is then the necessary gilding of a disagreeable pill. *L'aimable*† consists in a thousand of these little things aggregately. It is the *suaviter in modo*,‡ which I have so often recommended to you.

A man of the best parts, and the greatest learning, if he does not know the world by his own experience and observation, will be very absurd, and consequently very unwelcome, in company. He may say very good things; but they will probably be so ill-timed, misplaced, or improperly addressed, that he had much better hold his tongue. Full of his own matter, and uninformed of, or inattentive to the particular circumstances and situations of the

---

* Softness.
† Amiableness—loveliness.
‡ Gentleness in the manner.

company, he vents it indiscriminately; he puts some people out of countenance; he shocks others: and frightens all, who dread what may come out next. The most general rule that I can give you for the world, and of which your experience will convince you of the truth, is, never to give the tone to the company, but to take it from them; and to labour more to put them in conceit with themselves, than to make them admire you. Those whom you can make to like themselves better, will, I promise you, like you very well.

Address and manners, with weak persons, who are actually three-fourths of the world, are every thing; and even people of the best understanding, are taken in by them. Where the heart is not won, and the eye pleased, the mind will seldom be on our side.

Do not forget, that the desire of pleasing makes a man agreeable, or unwelcome, to those with whom he converses, according to the motive from which that inclination seems to flow. If your concern for pleasing others, arise from an innate benevolence, it never fails of success; if from vanity to excel, its disappointment is no less certain. What we call an agreeable man, is he who is endowed with a natural bent to do acceptable things from the delight he takes in them merely as such; and the affectation of that character is what constitutes a fop. Under one of these characters, you must make your future figure, and it remains with yourself to make the choice.

Avoir du monde* is, in my opinion, a very

---

* To have a fashionable air.

just and happy expression, for having address, manners, and for knowing how to behave properly in all companies. Without them, the best parts are inefficient, civility is absurd, and freedom offensive. A profound student, rusting in his cell at Oxford or Cambridge, will reason admirably well upon the nature of man; will profoundly analyse the head, the heart, the reason, the will, the passions, the senses, the sentiments, and all those subdivisions of we know not what; and yet, unfortunately, he knows nothing of man: for he hath not lived with him; and is ignorant of all the various modes, habits, prejudices, and tastes, that always influence and often determine him. He views man, as he does colours in Sir Isaac Newton's prism, where only capital ones are seen; but an experienced dyer knows all their various shades and gradations, together with the result of their several mixtures. Few men are of one plain, decided colour; most are mixed, shaded, and blended; and vary as much in different situations, as changeable silks do in different lights. The man *qui a du monde**
knows all this, from his own experience and observation: the cloistered philosopher knows nothing of it, from his own theory; his practice is absurd and improper; and he acts as awkwardly as a man would dance who had never seen others dance, nor learned of a dancing-master; but who had only studied the notes by which dances are now pricked down, as well as tunes. Strong minds have undoubtedly an ascendent over weak ones, as Galagai Maréchale d'Ancre very justly observed, when,

---

* Who has a fashionable air.

to the disgrace and reproach of those times,
she was executed, for having governed Mary
of Medicis, by the arts of witchcraft and ma-
gic. But then, ascendency is to be gained by
degrees, and by those arts only which are
taught by experience and a knowledge of the
world; for few are mean enough to be bullied,
though most are weak enough to be bubbled.
I have often seen people of superior, governed
by people of much inferior parts, without
knowing or even suspecting that they were
so governed. This can happen only when
those people of inferior parts, have more
worldly dexterity and experience, than those
they govern. They see the weak and unguarded part, and apply to it: they take it,
and all the rest follows.

This knowledge of the world teaches us,
more particularly, two things, both of which
are of infinite consequence, and to neither of
which nature inclines us; I mean the command of our temper, and our countenance.
A man who has no *monde*[*] is inflamed with
anger, or annihilated with shame, at every
disagreeable incident: the one makes him act
and talk like a madman, the other makes him
look like a fool. But a man who has *du monde*,
seems not to understand what he cannot or
ought not to resent. If he makes a slip himself, he recovers it by his coolness, instead of
plunging deeper, by his confusion, like a
stumbling horse. He is firm, but gentle; and
practices that most excellent maxim, *suavitèr
in modo, fortitèr in re.*[†] People, unused to

---

[*] Air—address.
[†] Gently in the manner—with firmness in
the execution.

the world, have babbling countenances; and
are unskilful enough to show what they have
sense enough not to tell. In the course of the
world, a man must very often put on an easy,
frank countenance, upon very disagreeable
situations. This may, nay, must be done,
without falsehood and treachery. It must go
no farther than politeness and manners, and
must stop short of assurances and professions
of simulated friendship. Good manners, to
those one does not love, are no more a breach
of truth, than is " your humble servant" at the
bottom of a challenge: they are universally
agreed upon, and understood to be things of
course. They are necessary guards of the
decency and peace of society: they must act
only defensively; and then not with arms
poisoned with perfidy. Truth, but not the
whole truth, must be the invariable principle
of every man, who hath either religion, honour, or prudence. Those who violate it may
be cunning, but they are not able. Lies and
perfidy are the refuge of fools and cowards.

In short, learning and erudition, without
good-breeding, is tiresome and pedantic: and
an ill bred man is as unfit for good company
as he will be unwelcome in it. Nay, he is full
as unfit for business, as for company. Make,
then, good breeding a principal object of your
thoughts and actions. Be particularly observ-
ant of the behaviour and manners of such as
are distinguished by their politeness, and endeavour to imitate them; and be persuaded,
that good breeding is, to all worldly qualifications, what charity is to all Christian virtues;
it adorns merit, and often covers the want
of it.

GOOD NATURE AND GOOD HUMOUR.

No society or conversation can be maintained in the world, without GOOD NATURE, or something that must resemble it, and supply its place. Good breeding is properly good-nature, gracefully displayed; and without it, it is only a kind of artificial humanity.

Good nature is more agreeable in conversation than wit; and is certain to make its possessor more beloved. It gives an air to the countenance, more amiable and commanding than beauty itself, and makes even folly and impertinence supportable. There is nothing, therefore, that we ought more to encourage, in ourselves, or others, than this happy temperament of mind.

Can any thing be more worthy of our labour, than to acquire a disposition to be pleased, and to place ourselves in a constant aptitude for the satisfactions of our being? Instead of this, you hardly see a man who is not uneasy, whose nature is not soured and ruffled in proportion to his advancement in the arts of life. An affected delicacy is the common improvement we meet with, in those who have pretensions to superior refinement. Such people are valetudinarians in society; and should no more come into company, than sick people into the air.

It is a wonderful thing, that so many persons, putting in claims to good breeding, should think of carrying the spleen into company, and entertaining those with whom they converse with a history of their pains, head-aches, and ill-treatment. This is, of all others, the meanest help to social happiness; and a man must have a very mean opinion of himself, who, on having detailed his grievances, is accosted by asking the news. Mutual good humour is a dress in which we ought to appear, whenever we meet; and we ought to make no mention of ourselves, unless it be in matters wherein our friends ought to rejoice. There is no real life, but cheerful life; therefore valetudinarians should be sworn, before they enter into company, not to say a word of themselves, until the meeting breaks up.

Whatever we do, we should keep up the cheerfulness of our spirits, and never let them sink below an inclination to be pleased. Fortune will give us disappointments enough, and nature is attended with infirmities enough, without our adding to the unhappy side of our account, by our spleen or ill-humour.

Study, then, to maintain a good humoured and cheerful temper. Rather aim at cheerfulness than mirth; at least, acquire a disposition to receive and give satisfaction. Without this, pretensions to breeding are unfounded; the finest things that can be said or done, will make you only a very successful mimic of genuine good breeding.

If you would have the *thing*, rather than the *name*, be assured you must struggle against every vicious propensity. Nothing but vice ought to ruffle the temper; as nothing but guilt can reasonably deprive us of a cheerful habit. None who live in a state of vice, can expect to be favoured with evenness and tranquillity of mind.

Do not suppose that I mean to make you gloomy, when I recommend a strict attention to your morals, as absolutely necessary to a respectable figure in life. You know I am no stoic; but I am serious, when I assure you, that vice is an enemy to inward tranquillity; and where this is not, it is impossible to appear, for any length of time, to advantage.

My object is to promote cheerfulness, not to suppress it. Carry with you, if you choose, into company, all the gaiety and spirits, but as little of the giddiness of youth as you can. The former will charm; but the latter will often, though innocently, implacably offend. Inform yourself of the characters and situations of the company, before you indulge in what your imagination may prompt you to say. There are, in all companies, more wrong heads than right ones; and many more who deserve, than who like censure. Should you therefore expatiate in the praise of some virtue, which some in company notoriously want; or declaim against any vice, with which others are notoriously infected; your reflections, however general and unapplied, will, by being applicable, be thought personal, and levelled at those people. This consideration points out to you, sufficiently, not to be suspicious and captious yourself, nor to suppose that things, because they may be, are therefore meant at you. The manners of well-bred people, secure one from those indirect and mean attacks; but if, by chance, a flippant woman, or a pert coxcomb, lets off any thing of that kind, it is much better not to seem to understand, than to reply to it.

Remember, that the wit, humour, and jokes, of most mixed companies, are local. They thrive in that particular soil, but will not, often, bear transplanting. Every company is differently circumstanced, has its particular cant and jargon; which may give occasion to wit and mirth, within that circle, but would seem flat and insipid in any other, and therefore will not bear repeating. Nothing makes a man look sillier, than a pleasantry, not relished, or not understood; and, if he meets with a profound silence, when he expected a general applause, or, what is worse, if he is desired to explain the *bon mot*,[*] his awkward and embarrassed situation is easier imagined than described. *A propos*[†] of repeating—take great care, never to repeat (I do not mean, here, the pleasantries) in one company, what you hear in another. Things, seemingly indifferent, may, by circulation, have much graver consequences, than you would imagine. Besides, there is a general tacit trust in conversation, by which a man is obliged not to report any thing out of it, though he be not immediately enjoined secrecy. A retailer of this kind is sure to draw himself into a thousand scrapes and discussions, and to be shily and uncomfortably received, wherever he goes.

GENTEEL CARRIAGE.

I MUST, from time to time, remind you of what I have often recommended, and of what you cannot attend to too much:—be graceful in your manners. The different effects of the

---

[*] Witticism.
[†] To the purpose—in this place.

same thing, said or done, when accompanied or deserted by graceful manners, is almost inconceivable. They prepare the way to the heart; and the heart has such an influence over the understanding, that it is worth while to engage it in our interest. From your own observation, reflect what a disagreeable impression an awkward address, a slovenly figure, an ungraceful manner of speaking, whether fluttering, muttering, monotony, or drawling an inattentive behaviour, &c. make upon you at first sight, in a stranger, and how they prejudice you against him, though, for aught you know, he may have great intrinsic sense and merit. And reflect, on the other hand, how much the opposites of all these things, prepossess you at first sight, in favour of those who enjoy them. You wish to find all good qualities in them, and are, in some degree, disappointed, if you do not. Observe, carefully, then, what displeases or pleases you in others: and be persuaded, that, in general, the same things will please or displease them in you.

Next to good breeding, is a genteel manner and carriage, wholly free from those ill habits and awkward actions, to which many very worthy persons are addicted.

A genteel manner of behaviour, how trifling soever it may seem, is of the utmost consequence in private life. Men of very inferior parts, have been esteemed, merely for their genteel carriage and good breeding; while sensible men have given disgust, for want of it. There is something or other that prepossesses us, at first sight, in favour of a well bred man, and makes us wish to like him.

There is a man whose moral character, deep

learning, and superior parts, I acknowledge, admire, and respect; but whom it is so impossible for me to love, that I am almost in a fever whenever I am in his company.* His figure (without being deformed) seems made to disgrace or ridicule the common structure of the human body. His legs and arms are never in the position, in which, according to the situation of his body, they ought to be; but constantly employed in committing acts of hostility upon the graces. He throws any where, but down his throat, whatever he means to drink; and only mangles what he means to carve. Inattentive to all the regards of social life, he mistimes or misplaces every thing. He disputes with heat, and indiscriminately; mindless of the rank, character, and situation of those with whom he disputes: absolutely ignorant of the several gradations of familiarity or respect, he is exactly the same to his superiors, his equals, and his inferiors; and therefore, by a necessary consequence, absurd to two of the three. Is it possible to love such a man? No. The utmost I can do for him, is to consider him as a respectable Hottentot.

An awkward address, ungraceful attitudes and actions, and a certain left-handedness, (if I may use that word) loudly proclaim low education, and low company. It is impossible to suppose that a man can have frequented good company, without having caught something, at least, of their air and motions. A new-raised man is distinguished, in a regiment, by his awkwardness; but he must be impenetrably dull, if, in a month or two's time, he can-

---

* The great Dr. Johnson.

not perform at least the common manual exercise, and look like a soldier. The very accoutrements of a man of fashion are grievous incumbrances to a vulgar man. He is at a loss what to do with his hat, when it is not upon his head. His clothes fit him so ill, and constrain him so much, that he seems rather their prisoner, than their proprietor. He presents himself in company, like a criminal in a court of justice; his very air condemns him: and people of fashion will no more connect themselves with the one, than people of character will with the other. This repulse drives and sinks him into low company; a gulf whence no man, after a certain age, ever emerged.

However trifling a genteel manner may sound, it is of very great consequence towards pleasing in private life, especially the women; whom, one time or other, you will think worth pleasing: and I have known many a man, from his awkwardness, give people such a dislike of him, at first, that all his merit could not get the better of it afterwards: whereas, a genteel manner preposses people in your favour, bends them towards you, and makes them wish to like you. Awkwardness can proceed from but two causes; either from not having kept good company, or from not having attended to it. As for your keeping good company, I will take care of that; do you take care to observe their ways and manners, and to form your own upon them. Attention is absolutely necessary for this, as indeed it is for every thing else; and a man without attention is not fit to live in the world.

When an awkward fellow first comes into a room, he attempts to bow, and his sword, if he wears one, goes between his legs, and nearly throws him down. Confused and ashamed, he stumbles to the upper end of the room, and seats himself in the very chair in which he should not. He there begins playing with his hat, which he presently drops; in recovering his hat, he lets fall his cane; and in picking up his cane, down goes his hat again: thus, it is a considerable time before he is adjusted. When his tea or coffee is handed to him, he spreads his handkerchief upon his knees, scalds his mouth, drops either the cup or the saucer, and spills the tea or coffee in his lap. At dinner, he is more uncommonly awkward. There he tucks his napkin through a button-hole, which tickles his chin, and occasions him to make a variety of wry faces; he seats himself upon the edge of the chair, at so great a distance from the table, that he frequently drops his meat between his plate and his mouth; he holds his knife, fork, and spoon, differently from other people; eats with his knife, to the manifest danger of his mouth; picks his teeth with his fork, rakes his mouth with his finger, and puts his spoon, which has been in his throat a dozen times, into the dish again. If he is to carve, he cannot hit the joint; but, in labouring to cut through the bone, splashes the sauce over every body's clothes. He generally daubs himself all over; his elbows are in the next person's plate, and he is up to the knuckles in soup and grease. If he drinks, it is with his mouth full, interrupting the whole company with, " To your good health, Sir," and, " My service to you ;" perhaps coughs in his glass, and besprinkles the whole table. Further, he has, perhaps, a number of disa-

greeable tricks; he snuffs up his nose, picks it
with his fingers, blows it, and looks into his
handkerchief, crams his hands first into his
bosom, and next into his breeches. In short,
he neither dresses nor acts, like any other person, but is particularly awkward, in every
thing he does. All this, I own, has nothing in
it criminal; but it is such an offence to good
manners and good breeding, that it is universally despised; it makes a man ridiculous, in
every company, and, of course, ought carefully to be avoided, by every one who would
wish to please.

From this picture of the ill-bred man, you
will easily discover that of the well-bred. You
may readily judge what you ought to do, when
told what you ought not to do; a little attention to the manners of those who have seen
the world, will make a proper behaviour habitual and familiar to you.

Actions that would otherwise be pleasing,
frequently become ridiculous, by your manner
of doing them. The worst bred man in Europe, if a lady let fall her fan, would certainly
take it up and give it to her: the best bred
man in Europe could do no more. The difference, however, would be considerable: the latter would please by doing it gracefully; the
former would be laughed at, for doing it awkwardly. I repeat it, and repeat it again, and
shall never cease repeating it to you—air,
manners, graces, style, elegancy, and all those
ornaments, must now be chief objects of your
attention; it is now, or never, that you must
acquire them.

Give all your motions, too, an air of *douceur*,*

---

* Softness.

which is directly the reverse of their present celerity and rapidity. Will you call this trouble? It will not be half an hour's trouble to you in a week's time. But, suppose it be; pray tell me, why did you give yourself the trouble of learning to dance? It is neither a religious, nor a moral, nor a civil duty. You must own, that you did it then singly to please, and you were right. Why do you wear fine clothes, and curl your hair? Both are troublesome: lank locks, and plain flimsy rags, are much easier. This, then, you also do, in order to please, and you do very right. But, then, reason and act consequentially; and endeavour to please in other things, too, still more essential, and without which the trouble you have taken in those is wholly thrown away. You are by no means ill-natured, and would you then most unjustly be reckoned so?

The manner of doing things, is often more important than the things themselves; and the very same thing may become either pleasing, or offensive, by the manner of saying or doing it. *Materiam superabat apus,** is often said of works of sculpture; where, though the materials were valuable, as silver, gold, &c. the workmanship was still more so. This holds true applied to manners; which adorn whatever knowledge or parts people may have; and even make a greater impression, upon nine in ten of mankind, than the intrinsic value of the materials. On the other hand, remember, that what Horace says of good writing, is justly applicable to those who would

---

* The workmanship surpassed the materials.

C

make a good figure in courts, and distinguish themselves in the shining parts of life; *Sapere principium et fons.** A man, who, without a good fund of knowledge and parts, adopts a court life, makes the most ridiculous figure imaginable. He is a machine, little superior to the court clock; and, as this points out the hours, he points out the frivolous employment of them. He is, at most, a comment upon the clock; and, according to the hours that it strikes, tells you, now it is levee, now dinner. now supper time, &c. The end which I propose by your education, and which, (if you please) I shall certainly attain, is to unite in you all the knowledge of a scholar, with the manners of a courtier; and to join, what is seldom joined in any of my countrymen, books and the world. They are commonly twenty years old, before they have spoken to any one above their school-master and the fellows of their college. If they happen to have learning, it is only Greek and Latin; but not one word of modern history, or modern languages. Thus prepared, they go abroad, as they call it: but, in truth, they stay at home all that time; for, being very awkward, confoundedly ashamed, and not speaking the languages, they go into no foreign company, at least none good; but dine and sup with one another, only, at a tavern. Such examples, I am sure, you will not imitate, but even carefully avoid. You will always take care to keep the best company in the place where you are, which is the only use of travelling; and (by the way)

---

* To be wise, is the chief object, and the source of happiness.

the pleasures of a gentleman are to be found only in the best company; for, that riot, which low company, most falsely and impudently call pleasure, is only the sensuality of the swine.

You may also know a well bred person, by his manner of sitting. Ashamed and confused, the awkward man sits in his chair stiff and bolt upright, whereas the man of fashion, is easy in every position: instead of lolling or lounging as he sits, he leans with elegance, and by varying his attitudes, shows that he has been used to good company.

Take particular care that the motions of your hands and arms be easy and graceful; for the genteelness of a man consists more in them than in any thing else. Desire some women to tell you of any little awkwardness that they observe in your carriage; they are the best judges of those things: if they are satisfied, the men will be so too.

In short, you cannot conceive how advantageous a graceful carriage and a pleasing address are, upon all occasions. They ensnare the affections, steal a prepossession in our favour, and play about the heart, until they engage it.

Now to acquire a graceful air, you must attend to your dancing: no one can either sit, stand, or walk well, unless he dances well. In learning to dance, be particularly attentive to the motion of your arms; for a stiffness in the wrist will make any man look awkward. If a man walks well, presents himself well in company, wears his hat well, moves his head properly and his arms gracefully, it is almost all that is necessary.

There is also an awkwardness in speech, that naturally falls under this head, and ought to be, and may be guarded against; such as forgetting names, and mistaking one name for another. To speak of Mr. What-d'ye-call-him, or You-know-who, Mrs. Thingum, What's-her-name, or How-d'ye-call-her, is exceedingly awkward and vulgar. It is the same, to address people by improper titles, as *sir* for *my lord;* to begin a story, without being able to finish it, and break off in the middle, with " I have forgot the rest."

Our voice and manner of speaking should likewise be attended to. Some mumble over their words, so as not to be intelligible; and others speak so fast, as not to be understood: and, in doing this, will sputter and spit in your face; some bawl, as if they were speaking to the deaf; others speak so low, as scarcely to be heard; and many put their face so close to yours, as to offend you with their breath. All these habits are horrid and disgusting; but may easily be corrected, with care. They are the vulgar characteristics of a low bred man: or are proofs that very little pains have been bestowed upon his education. In short, an attention to these little matters, are of greater importance, than you are aware of: many a sensible man, having lost ground for want of these little graces, and many a one, possessed of these perfections alone, having made his way through life, that otherwise would not have been noticed.

Be careful of contracting awkward habits, such as biting your nails, picking your nose, scratching your head, drumming with your feet, coughing to clear your throat, sighing, &c.; all which are disgusting to an extreme.

These, and many other very disagreeable
habits, are owing to *mauvaise honte,** at people's first setting out in the world. They are
ashamed in company, and so disconcerted,
that they do not know what they do, and try a
thousand tricks to keep themselves in countenance; which tricks afterwards grow habitual.
Some put their fingers in their nose, others
scratch their head, others twirl their hats; in
short, every awkward ill bred body has his
trick. But the frequency does not justify the
thing; and all these vulgar habits and this
awkwardness, though not criminal, indeed, are
most carefully to be guarded against; as they
are great bars in the way of the art of pleasing.
Remember, that to please, is almost to prevail,
or at least a necessary previous step to it.
You, who have your fortune to make, should
more particularly study this art.

Mauvaise honte not only hinders young people from making a great many friends, but
makes them a great many enemies. They are
ashamed of doing the thing that they know to
be right, and would otherwise do, for fear of
the momentary laugh of some fine gentleman
or lady. I have been in this case, and have
often wished an obscure acquaintance absent,
for meeting and taking notice of me, when I
was in what I thought and called fine company. I have returned his notice shily, awkwardly, and consequently offensively, for fear
of a momentary joke; not considering, as I
ought to have done, that the very people who
would have joked upon me at first, would
have esteemed me the more for it afterwards.

---

* Ill-timed shame—excessive bashfulness.

A rule is best explained by example. Suppose you were walking in the Thuilleries, with some fine folks, and that you should unexpectedly meet your old acquaintance, little crooked Grierson; what would you do? I will tell you what you should do, by telling you what I would now do, in that case, myself. I would run up to him, and embrace him; say some kind things to him, and then return to my company. There I should be immediately asked: *Mais qu'est ce que c'est donc que ce petit sapajou que vous avez embrassé si tendrement? Pour cela l'accolade a été charmante;** with a great deal more festivity of that sort. To this, I should answer, without being the least ashamed, but *en badinant:*† *O! je ne vous dirai pas qui c'est; c'est un petit ami que je tiens incognito, qui a son merite, et qui, à force d'être connu, fait oublier sa figure. Que me donnérez-vous, et je vous le présenterai?*‡ And then, with a little more seriousness, I would add, *Mais d'ailleurs c'est que je ne désavoue jamais mes connoissances, à cause de leur état ou de leur figure. Il faut avoir bien peu de sentiments pour le faire.*‖ This would at

---

* But who is that little marmouset, that you have been embracing so tenderly? That was a delightful hug!

† Playfully.

‡ O! I won't tell you who it is: he is a young friend, whom I keep unknown, who is a person of merit, and with whom when one is acquainted, one forgets his appearance.—But, what will you give me, if I introduce you to him?

‖ But I never disown my acquaintances, on

once put an end to that momentary pleasantry, and give them all a better opinion of me, than they had before. Pursue steadily, in a word, and without fear or shame, whatever your reason tells you is right, and what you see is practised by people of more experience than yourself, and of established characters of good sense and good breeding.

If people had no vices but their own, few would have so many as they have. For my own part, I would sooner wear other people's clothes, than their vices; and they would sit upon me just as well. I hope you will have none; but if ever you have, I beg, at least, they may be all your own. Vices of adoption are, above all others, the most disgraceful and unpardonable. There are degrees in vices, as well as in virtues; and I must do my countrymen the justice to say, they generally take their vices in the lowest degree. Their gallantry is the infamous mean debauchery of stews, justly attended and rewarded by the loss of their health, as well as their character. Their pleasures of the table end in beastly drunkenness, low riot, broken windows, and very often (as they well deserve) broken bones. They game, for the sake of the vice, not of the amusement; and therefore carry it to excess; undo, or are undone by their companions.

As for the *mauvaise honte*, I hope you are above it. Your figure is like other people's; I suppose you will take care that your dress shall be so too, and avoid any singularity.

account of their circumstances, or their appearance. I should have very little feeling, were I to do so.

What then should you be ashamed of? Why
not go into a mixed company, with as much
ease, and as little concern, as you would go
into your own room? Vice and ignorance
are the only things I know, of which one
ought to be ashamed: keep but clear of them,
and you may go any where, without fear or
concern. I have known some people, who,
from feeling the pain and inconveniences of
this *mauvaise honte*, have rushed into the
other extreme, and turned impudent; as cowards sometimes grow desperate, from the excess of danger: but this, too, is carefully to be
avoided; there being nothing more generally
shocking than impudence. The medium between these two extremes, marks out the well
bred man. He feels himself firm and easy, in
all companies; is modest without being bashful, and steady without being impudent: if he
is a stranger, he observes, with care, the manners and ways of the people the most esteemed at that place, and conforms to them, with
complaisance. Instead of finding fault with
the customs of that place, and telling the people that the English are a thousand times better (as my countrymen are very apt to do) he
commends their table, their dress, their
houses, and their manners, whenever he sees
occasion for commendation. This degree of
complaisance, is neither criminal nor abject;
and is but a small price to pay for the good
will and affection of the people with whom
you converse. As the generality of people
are weak enough to be pleased with these little things, those who refuse to please them, so
cheaply, are, in my mind, weaker than they.
 Do not mistake, and think that these graces,

which I so often and so earnestly recommend, should accompany only important transactions, and be worn only *les jours de gala:** no; they should, if possible, accompany even the least thing that you do or say; for if you neglect them, in little things, they will leave you in great ones. I should, for instance, be extremely concerned to see you even drink a cup of coffee ungracefully, and slop yourself with it, by your awkward manner of holding it; nor should I like to see your coat buttoned, or shoes buckled awry. But I should be outrageous, if I heard you mutter your words unintelligibly, stammer in your speech, or hesitate, misplace, and mistake in your narrations: and I should run away from you, with greater rapidity, if possible, than I should now run to embrace you, if I found you destitute of all those graces which I have set my heart upon making you one day, *omnibus ornatum excellere rebus.*†

ART OF PLEASING.

HAVING interwoven occasional remarks upon the ART OF PLEASING, in some of my former letters, I shall now direct your attention professedly to this subject.

Although we generally agree as to what it is to be complaisant, it is hard to define it. I take it to consist in a respectful attention to others, adapted, in its degree, to the quality of the object. It is an enviable secret possessed

---

* Holidays.
† Accomplished in all things.

by few, but which renders those few the favourites of mankind.

It is a very old, and very true maxim, that
those kings reign the most secure, and the
most absolute, who reign in the hearts of
their people. Their popularity is a better
guard than their army; and the affections of
their subjects a better pledge of their obedience, than their fears. This rule is, in proportion, fully as true, though upon a different
scale, with regard to private people. A man
who possesses that great art of pleasing universally, and of gaining the affections of those
with whom he converses, possesses a strength,
which nothing else can give him: a strength
which facilitates and helps his rise; and
which, in case of accidents, breaks his fall.
Few people, of your age, sufficiently consider
this great point of popularity; and, when they
grow older and wiser, they strive, in vain, to
recover what they lost by their negligence.
There are three principal causes that hinder
them from acquiring this useful strength:
pride, inattention, and *mauvaise honte*. Of
the first, I will not, I cannot suspect you: it is
too much below your understanding. You
cannot, and I am sure you do not, think yourself superior, by nature, to the Savoyard who
cleans your room, or the footman who cleans
your shoes; but you may rejoice, and with
reason, at the difference that Providence has
made in your favour. Enjoy all those advantages; but without insulting people who are
unfortunate enough to want them; or even
doing any thing unnecessarily that may remind them of that want. For my own part,
I am more upon my guard as to my behaviour

to my servants, and others who are called my
inferiors, than I am towards my equals; for
fear of being suspected of that mean and ungenerous sentiment, of desiring to make others
feel that difference, which fortune has, and
perhaps, too, undeservedly, made between us.
Young people do not enough attend to this;
but falsely imagine that the imperative mood,
and a rough tone of authority and decision, are
indications of spirit and courage. Inattention
is always looked upon, though sometimes unjustly, as the effect of pride and contempt;
and, where it is thought so, is never forgiven.
In this article, young people are generally exceedingly to blame, and offend extremely.
Their whole attention is engrossed by their
particular set of acquaintance, and by some
few glaring and exalted objects of rank, beauty, or parts: all the rest they think so little
worth their care, that they neglect even common civility towards them. I will frankly
confess, that this was one of my great faults,
when I was of your age. Very attentive to
please that narrow court circle in which I
stood enchanted, I considered every thing else
as *bourgeois*,* and unworthy of common civility. I paid my court assiduously and skilfully
enough to shining and distinguished figures,
such as ministers, wits, and beauties; but then
I most absurdly and imprudently neglected,
and consequently offended, all others. By this
folly, I made myself a thousand enemies, of
both sexes; who, though I thought them very
insignificant, found means to hurt me essentially, where I wanted to recommend myself

---

* Citizens—tradesmen.

the most. I was thought proud, though I was only imprudent. A general easy civility and attention, to the common run of ugly women, and of middling men, both which I sillily thought, called, and treated as odd people, would have made me as many friends as, by the contrary conduct, I made myself enemies. All this too was *à pure perte;** for I might equally, and even more successfully, have made my court where I had particular views to gratify. I will allow, that this task is often very unpleasant; and that one pays, with some unwillingness, that tribute of attention to dull and tedious men, and to old and ugly women; but it is the lowest price of popularity and general applause, which are very well worth purchasing, were they much dearer. I conclude this head with this advice: gain, by particular assiduity and address, the men and women you want; and, by a universal civility and attention, please every body, so far as to have their good word, if not their good will; or, at least, as to secure a partial neutrality. Know every one; and endeavour (as far as you can, with good conscience) to please every one; I mean exteriorly; for fundamentally it is impossible. Modes and manners vary in different places, and at different times: you must know them, and accommodate yourself to them. The great usage of the world, the knowledge of characters, is what you now want.

The art of pleasing is a very necessary one to possess; but a very difficult one to acquire. It can hardly be reduced to rules; and your own good sense and observation, will teach

---

* A clear disadvantage.

you more of it, than I can. Do as you would be done by, is the surest method that I know of pleasing. Observe carefully what pleases you in others; and probably the same things in you will please others. If you are pleased with the complaisance and attention of others to you, depend upon it, the same complaisance and attention, on your part, will equally please them. Take the tone of the company that you are in, and do not pretend to give it: be serious or gay, as you find the present humour of the company: this is an attention due from every individual to the majority. Do not tell stories in company; there is nothing more tedious and disagreeable. If, by chance, you know a very short story, and exceedingly applicable to the present subject of conversation, tell it in as few words as possible; and even then, throw out that you do not love to tell stories: but that the shortness of it tempted you. Of all things, banish egotism out of your conversation, and never think of entertaining people with your own personal concerns, or private affairs: though they are interesting to you, they are tedious and impertinent to every body else; besides, that one cannot keep one's own private affairs too secret. Whatever you think your own excellences may be, do not affectedly display them in company; nor labour, as many people do, to give that turn to the conversation, which may supply you with an opportunity of exhibiting them. they are real, they will infallibly be discovered, without your pointing them out yourself; and with much more advantage.

Of all the various ingredients, that compose the useful and necessary art of pleasing, none

is so effectual and engaging, as that gentleness, that *douceur** of countenance and manners, to which you are no stranger, though a
sworn enemy.   Other people take great pains
to conceal or disguise their natural imperfections.   Some, by the make of their clothes,
and other arts, endeavour to conceal the defects of their shape; women, who unfortunately have natural bad complexions, lay on
good ones; and both men and women, upon
whom unkind nature has inflicted a surliness
and ferocity of countenance, do at least all
they can, though often without success, to
soften and mitigate it: they aim at smiles,
though often, in the attempt, like the devil in
Milton, they *grin horribly a ghastly smile.*
But you are the only person I ever knew, in
the whole course of my life, that not only dis-
dains, but absolutely rejects and disguises a
great advantage that nature has kindly granted. You easily guess that I mean *countenance;*
for she has given you a very pleasing one;
but you beg to be excused, you will not accept
it; on the contrary, take singular pains to put
on the most *funeste,*† forbidding, and unpleas-
ing one, that can possibly be imagined.   This,
one would think impossible, but you know it
to be true.   If you imagine that it gives you a
manly, thoughtful, and decisive air, as some,
though very few of your countrymen do, you
are exceedingly mistaken; for it is at best the
air of a German corporal, part of whose exercise is to look fierce.

Without the desire and attention necessary

---

* Softness, mildness.
† Mournful, gloomy.

to please, you never can please. *Nullum nu-men abest, si sit prudentia** is unquestionably true, with regard to every thing, except poe-try; and I am very sure that any man of com-mon understanding may, by proper culture, care, attention, and labour, make himself whatever he pleases, except a good poet.

With a desire of pleasing every body, I came by degrees to please some; and, I can assure you, that what little figure I have made in the world, has been much more owing to that desire I had of pleasing universally, than to any intrinsic merit or sound know-ledge of which I might ever have been master.

The greatest favours may be done so awk-wardly and bunglingly, as to offend; and disa-greeable things may be done so agreeably, as almost to oblige. Endeavour to acquire this great secret. It exists, it is to be found, and is worth a great deal more than the grand secret of the alchymists would be, if it were, as it is not, to be found.

The knowledge of a scholar, the courage of a hero, and the virtue of a stoic, will be ad-mired; but, if the knowledge be accompanied with arrogance, the courage with ferocity, and the virtue with inflexible severity, the man will never be loved.

Civility, which is a disposition to accommo-date and oblige others, is essentially the same, in every country: but, good breeding, as it is called, which is the manner of exerting that disposition, is different in almost every coun-try, and merely local; and every man of sense imitates and conforms to that local good breed-

* No protecting power is wanting, if pru-dence be but employed.

ing of the place which he is at. A conformity
and flexibility of manners is necessary, in the
course of the world; that is, with regard to
all things which are not wrong in themselves.
The *versatile ingenium** is the most useful of
all. It can turn itself instantly from one object to another, assuming the proper manner
for each. It can be serious with the grave,
cheerful with the gay, and trifling with the
frivolous. Endeavour, by all means, to acquire
this talent, for it is a very great one. Do not
mistake me, and think that I mean to recommend to you abject and criminal flattery: no :
flatter nobody's vices or crimes; on the contrary, abhor and discourage them. But there
is no living in the world, without a complaisant indulgence for people's innocent weaknesses.

All these engaging and endearing accomplishments, are mechanical, and to be acquired by care and observation, as easily as
turning, or any mechanical trade. A common country fellow, taken from the plough,
and enlisted in an old corps, soon lays aside
his shambling gait, his slouching air, his
clumsy and awkward motions, and acquires
the martial air, the regular motions, and the
whole exercise of the corps, and particularly
of his right and left hand man. How so? Not
from his parts, which were just the same before, as after, he was enlisted; but either
from a commendable ambition of being like,
and equal to those with whom he is to live;
or else from the fear of being punished, for not
being so. If, then, both or either of these mo-

---

* Accommodating disposition—fertility of
expedients.

tives change such a fellow, in about six months' time, to such a degree, as that he is not to be known again, how much stronger should both these motives be with you, to acquire, in the utmost perfection, the whole exercise of the people of fashion, with whom you are to live all your life? Ambition should make you resolve to be at least their equal in that exercise; as well as the fear of punishment, which most inevitably will attend the want of it. By that exercise, I mean the air, the manners, the graces, and the style, of people of fashion.

There is one maxim which you cannot study too much:—It is, *suavitèr in modo, fortitèr in re.** I do not know any one rule so unexceptionably useful and necessary, in every part of life. I shall therefore take it for my text, to-day; and, as old men love preaching, and I have some right to preach to you, I here present you with my sermon upon these words. To proceed, then, regularly and *pulpitically;* I will first show you, my beloved! the necessary connexion of the two members of my text—*suavitèr in modo, fortitèr in re.* In the next place, I shall set forth the advantages and utility resulting from a strict observance of the precept contained in my text; and conclude with an application of the whole.

The *suavitèr in modo,* alone, would degenerate and sink into a mean, timid complaisance and passiveness, if not supported and dignified by the *fortitèr in re;* which would also run into impetuosity and brutality, if not tempered

* Gently in the manner—with firmness in the execution.

and softened by the *suavitèr in modo.* However, they are seldom united. The warm, choleric man, with strong animal spirits, despises the *suavitèr in modo*, and thinks to carry all before him, by the *fortitèr in re.* He may, possibly, by great accident, now and then succeed, when he has only weak and timid people to deal with; but his general fate will be, to shock, offend, be hated, and fail. On the other hand, the cunning, crafty man, thinks to gain all his ends by the *suavitèr in modo*, only: he becomes all things to all men; he seems to have no opinion of his own, and servilely adopts the present opinion of the present person; he insinuates himself only into the esteem of fools, but is soon detected, and surely despised by every body else. The wise man, alone, (who differs as much from the cunning, as from the choleric) joins the *suavitèr in modo* with the *fortitèr in re.*

There is a *bienséance*,* also, with regard to people of the lowest degree: a gentleman observes it with his footman, even with a beggar in the street. He considers them as objects of compassion, not of insult; he speaks to neither *d'un ton brusque*,† but corrects the one coolly, and refuses the other with humanity. There is no one occasion in the world, in which *le ton brusque* is becoming a gentleman. In short, *les bienséances*‡ are another word for *manners*, and extend to every part of life.— They are propriety; the Graces should attend, to complete them: the Graces enable us to do

---

* Decorum.   † In a rough tone.
          ‡ The decencies.

genteely and pleasingly what *les bienséances* require to be done at all. The latter are an obligation, upon every man; the former are an infinite advantage and ornament, to any man.

If you are in authority, and have a right to command, your commands delivered *suaviter in modo* will be willingly, cheerfully and consequently, well obeyed; whereas, if given only *fortiter*, that is brutally, they will rather, as Tacitus says, be interpreted than executed. For my own part, if I bid my footman bring me a glass of wine, in a rough, insulting manner, I should expect that, in obeying me, he would contrive to spill some of it upon me; and, I am sure, I should deserve it. A cool, steady resolution, should show, that, where you have a right to command, you will be obeyed; but, at the same time, a gentleness in the manner of enforcing that obedience, should make it a cheerful one, and soften, as much as possible, the mortifying consciousness of inferiority. If you are to ask a favour, or even to solicit your due, you must do it *suaviter in modo*, or you will give those, who have a mind to refuse you either, a pretence to do it, by resenting the manner; but, on the other hand, you must, by a steady perseverance, and decent tenaciousness, show the *fortiter in re*. The right motives are seldom the true ones of men's actions, especially of kings, ministers, and people in high stations, who often give to importunity and fear, what they would refuse to justice or to merit. By the *suaviter in modo* engage their hearts, if you can; at least, prevent the pretence of offence: but take care to show enough of the *fortiter in re*, to extort, from their love of ease, or their fear, what you

might in vain hope for from their justice or
good nature. People in high life are hardened
to the wants and distresses of mankind, as sur-
geons are to their bodily pains: they see and
hear them all day long, and even of so many
simulated cases, that they do not know which
are real, and which not. Other sentiments
are therefore to be applied, than those of mere
humanity and justice. Their favour must be
captivated, by the *suaviter in modo*: their love
of ease disturbed, by unwearied importunity;
or their fears wrought upon by a decent inti-
mation of implacable, cool resentment. This
is the true *fortiter in re.* This precept is the
only way I know in the world, of being loved,
without being despised, and feared without
being hated. It constitutes the dignity of character, which every wise man must endeavour
to establish.

It is not enough, not to be rude: you should
be civil, and distinguished for your good breeding. The first principle of this good breeding
is, never to say any thing that you think can
be disagreeable to any body in company; but,
on the contrary, you should endeavour to say
what will be agreeable to them; and that in an
easy and natural manner, without seeming to
study for compliments. There is likewise
such a thing as a civil look and a rude look ;
and you should look civil, as well as be so; for
if, while you are saying a civil thing, you look
gruff and surly, as most country bumpkins do,
nobody will be obliged to you, for a civility
that seemed to come so unwillingly. If you
have occasion to contradict any one, or to set
him right from a mistake, it would be very
brutal to say, "That is not so; I know bet-

ter;" or, "You are out:" but you should
say, with a civil look, "I beg your pardon, I
believe you mistake;" or, "If I may take
the liberty of contradicting you, I believe it
is so and so:" for, though you may know a
thing better than other people, yet it is very
shocking to tell them so, directly, without
something to soften it; but, remember, particularly, that, whatever you say or do, with
ever so civil an intention, a great deal consists
in the manner and the look, which must be
genteel, easy, and natural, and is easier to be
felt, than described.

Civility is particularly due to all women;
and remember, that no provocation whatsoever
can justify any man in not being civil to every
woman; and the greatest man in England
would justly be reckoned a brute, if he was
not civil to the meanest woman. It is due to
their sex, and is the only protection they have
against the superior strength of ours. Observe the best and most well bred of the
French people, how agreeably they insinuate
little civilities in their conversation. They
think it so essential, that they call an honest
and civil man by the same name, of *honnête homme;* and the Romans called civility
humanitas, as thinking it inseparable from humanity; and, depend upon it, that your reputation and success in the world, will, in a great
measure, depend upon the degree of good
breeding of which you are master. You cannot begin too early, to take that turn, in order
to make it natural and habitual; which it is to
very few Englishmen; who, neglecting it
while they are young, find out, too late, when
they are old, how necessary it is, and then
cannot rightly acquire it.

You will find, in most good company, some
people, who keep their place there only by a
contemptible title enough; these are what we
call very good natured fellows, and the French
*bons diables.** The truth is, they are people
without any parts or fancy; and who, having
no will of their own, readily assent to, concur
in, and applaud, whatever is said or done in
the company; and adopt, with the same alacrity, the most virtuous, or the most criminal,
the wisest or the silliest scheme, that happens
to be entertained by the majority of the company. This foolish, and often criminal complaisance, flows from a foolish cause—the want
of any other merit. I hope you will hold your
place in company by a nobler tenure; and that
you will hold it (you can bear a quibble, I believe,
yet) *in capite.*† Have a will and an opinion of
your own, and steadily adhere to them; but,
then, do it with good humour, good breeding,
and (if you have it) with urbanity; for you have
not beard enough, either to preach or censure.

All other kinds of complaisance are not only
blameless, but necessary in good company.
Not to seem to perceive the little weaknesses,
and the idle but innocent affectations of the
company, is not only very allowable, but in
truth, a sort of polite duty. They will be
pleased with you, if you do; and will certainly not be reformed by you, if you do not.
For instance, you will find, in every group of
company, two principal figures; viz. the fine
lady and the fine gentleman: who absolutely
give the law of wit and language, fashion and
taste, to the rest of that society. There is always a strict, and often, for the time being, a

---

* Pleasant devils.   † In chief.

tender alliance, between these two figures. The lady looks upon her empire as founded upon the divine right of beauty; (and fully as good a divine right it is, as any king, emperor, or pope, can pretend to;) she requires, and commonly meets with, unlimited, passive obedience. The gentleman has an equally indisputable title, in the department of courteous behaviour.

After all this, perhaps you will say that it is impossible to please every one. I grant it: but it does not follow that one should not therefore endeavour to please as many as one can. Nay, I will go farther, and admit that it is impossible for any man not to have some enemies. But this truth, from long experience, I assert, that he who has the most friends, and the fewest enemies, is the strongest; will rise the highest with the least envy; and fall, if he does fall, the gentlest, and the most pitied.

There is no one creature so obscure, so low, or so poor, who may not, by the strange and unaccountable changes and vicissitudes of human affairs, some way or other, and some time or other, become a useful friend, or a troublesome enemy, to the greatest and the richest.

By these means, you may and will very often be gainer,—you never can be a loser. Some people cannot gain upon themselves to be easy and civil to those who are either their rivals, competitors, or opposers; though, independently of those accidental circumstances, they would like and esteem them. They betray a shyness and an awkwardness in company with them; and catch at any little thing to expose them; so, from temporary and only occasional opponents, make them their personal enemies. This is exceedingly weak and detrimental; as, indeed, is all humour in business: which can be carried on successfully only by unadulterated good policy, and right reasoning. In such cases, I would be more particularly, and *noblement*,* civil, easy, and frank, with the man whose designs I traversed. This is commonly called generosity and magnanimity, but is, in truth, good sense and policy. The manner is often as important as the matter, sometimes more so; a favour may make an enemy, and an injury may make a friend, according to the different manner in which they are severally done. The countenance, the address, the words, the enunciation, the graces, add great efficacy to the *suaviter in modo*, and great dignity to the *fortiter in re*: and consequently they deserve the utmost attention.

From what has been said, I conclude, with this observation—That gentleness of manners, with firmness of mind, is a short, but full description of human perfection, on this side of religious and moral duties.

CLEANLINESS OF PERSON.

No one can please in company, however graceful his air, unless he be clean and neat in his person; a qualification which comes next to be considered.

Negligence of one's person, implies not only an insufferable indolence, but an indifference

---

* Politely.

whether we please or not. In others, it be-
:rays an insolence and affectation, arising from
a presumption, that they are sure of pleasing,
without having recourse to those means which
many are obliged to use.

We need only compare our ideas of a female
Hottentot and an English beauty, to be satisfied of this truth.

Beauty, without cleanliness, may excite
love, but it cannot secure it. An indifferent
person kept clean, will make more conquests,
than a beautiful slattern. We look upon age
itself, when clean, as on a piece of metal, kept
bright and smooth by wearing.

In a word, cleanliness, as it makes us more
agreeable to others, so it makes us easy in ourselves. It bears a strict analogy to purity of
mind; pure and unsullied impressions are
usually the first that are made on seeing persons remarkable for their cleanliness. Whatever motives may induce persons to neglect
their persons, the consequences are, disgust
and want of respect, in those with whom they
associate, and in themselves, uneasiness and
disease.

He who is not thoroughly clean in his person, will be offensive to all with whom he converses. A particular regard to the cleanliness
of your mouth, teeth, hands and nails, is but
common decency.

A foul mouth and unclean hands, are certain marks of vulgarity: the first is the cause
of an offensive breath, which nobody can bear,
and the last is declarative of dirty work. One
may always know a gentleman, by the state of
his hands and nails. The flesh, at the roots,
should be kept back so as to show the semi-

D

circles at the bottom of the nails; the edges of the nails should never be cut down below the ends of the fingers, nor should they be suffered to grow longer than the fingers. When the nails are cut down to the quick, it is a shrewd sign that the man is a mechanic, to whom long nails would be troublesome, or that he gets his bread by fiddling; and if they are longer than his finger ends and encircled with a black rim, it foretells he has been laboriously and meanly employed, and too fatigued to clean himself:—a good apology for want of cleanliness, in a mechanic, but the greatest disgrace that can attend a gentleman.

These things may appear too insignificant, to be mentioned; but when it is considered that a thousand little nameless things, which every one feels, but no one can describe, conspire to form that *whole* of pleasing, I hope you will not call them trifling. Besides, a clean shirt and a clean person are as necessary to health, as to prevent giving offence to other people. It is a maxim with me, which I have lived to see verified, that he who is negligent at twenty years of age, will be a sloven at forty, and intolerable at fifty.

DRESS.

NEATNESS of person, I observed, was as necessary as cleanliness; of course, some attention must be paid to your DRESS.

It must be confessed, that few things make a man appear more despicable, or prejudice others against him more strongly, than an awkward or pitiful dress. Had Tully himself pronounced one of his orations, with a blanket about him, perhaps more people would have laughed at his dress, than have admired his eloquence.

If there be absurdity in the fashion which regulates dress, it will discover more good sense, to conform, to a certain degree, than to resist and be pointed at as a sloven, or acquire a character for singularity; and the respect which we owe, both to others and to ourselves, forbids us to be either slovenly or singular.

In the first place, to neglect one's dress, is to affront all the female part of our acquaintance. The women, in particular, pay an attention to their dress; to neglect therefore yours will displease them, as it would be tacitly taxing them with vanity, and declaring that you thought them not worth that respect which every body else does: and, as I have mentioned before, as it is the women who stamp a young man's credit, in the fashionable world, if you do not make yourself agreeable to the women you will assuredly lose ground among the men.

Dress, as trifling as it may appear to a man of understanding, preposseses, on the first appearance, which is frequently decisive. Indeed, we may form some opinion of a man's sense and character from his dress. Any excess, in following the fashion, or any affectation in dress whatever, argues a weakness in the understanding.

There are few young fellows that do not display some character or another in this shape. But a man of sense carefully avoids any particular character in his dress: he is accurately clean, for his own sake; but all the rest is for other people's. He dresses as well, and in the same manner, as the people of sense and fashion in the place where he is. If he dresses better, as he thinks, that is, more than they, he is a fop; if he dresses worse, he is unpardonably negligent: but, of the two, I would rather have a young fellow too much, than too little dressed.

Whatever the world, or even philosophers, have affected to say of dress, you may rest assured they do not think it a matter of so much indifference as they pretend. Travel only a single day, with a slovenly garb, in the company of a well dressed man, and you will be convinced of the truth of this remark. Consult your own good taste, therefore, in your dress. Let that be the glass, at which you shall adjust and fit your apparel.

Dress yourself fine, where others are fine; and plain, where others are plain: but take care, always, that your clothes are well made, and fit you; otherwise they will give you a very awkward air. When you are once well dressed for the day, think no more of it afterwards; and, without any stiffness for fear of discomposing that dress, let all your motions be as easy and natural, as if you had no clothes on at all. So much for dress; which I maintain to be a thing of importance, in the polite world.

———

ELEGANCE OF EXPRESSION.

Having mentioned elegance of person, I will proceed to Elegance of Expression.

One or two qualifications alone do not complete the gentleman. It must be a union of many; and graceful speaking is as essential as gracefulness of person. Every man cannot be an harmonious speaker; a roughness or coarseness of voice may prevent it; but, if there are no natural imperfections, if a man does not stammer, or lisp, or has not lost his teeth, he may speak gracefully; nor will all these defects, if he has a mind to it, prevent him from speaking correctly.

No one can attend, with pleasure, to 'a bad speaker. One who tells his story ill, be it ever so important, will tire even the most patient. If you have been present at the performance of a good tragedy, you have doubtless been sensible of the good effects of a speech well delivered; how much it has interested and affected you; and, on the contrary, how much an ill spoken one has disgusted you. It is the same, in common conversation. He who speaks deliberately, distinctly, and correctly; he who makes use of the best words to express himself, and varies his voice according to the nature of the subject, will always please, while the thick or hasty speaker, he who mumbles out a set of ill chosen words, utters them ungrammatically, or with a dull monotony, will tire and disgust.

You must, certainly, in the course of your little experience, have felt the different effects of elegant and inelegant speaking. Do you not suffer, when people accost you in a stammering or hesitating manner ; in an untuneful voice, with false accents and cadences ; puzzling and blundering through solecisms, barbarisms, and vulgarisms ; misplacing even their bad words, and inverting all method? Does not this prejudice you against their matter, be it what it will; nay, even against their persons? I am sure it does me. On the other hand, do you not feel yourself inclined, prepossessed, nay, even engaged, in favour of those who address you in a directly contrary manner? The effects of a correct and adorned style, of method and perspicuity, are incredible towards persuasion; they often supply the want of reason and argument; but, when used in the support of reason and argument, they are irresistible. If you have the least defect in your elocution, take the utmost care and pains to correct it. Do not neglect your style, in whatever language you speak, or whomsoever you speak to, were it your footman. Seek always for the best words, and the happiest expressions, you can find. Do not content yourself with being barely understood; but adorn your thoughts, and dress them as you would your person; which, however well proportioned it might be, it would be very improper and indecent to exhibit naked, or even worse dressed than people of your rank are.

Oratory, with all its graces, that of enunciation in particular, is full as necessary, in our government, as it ever was in Greece or Rome. No man can make a fortune or a figure in this country, without speaking, and speaking well, in public. If you will persuade, you must first please; and if you will please, you must tune your voice to harmony, you must articulate every syllable distinctly, your emphases and cadences must be strongly and properly marked, and the whole together must be graceful and engaging: if you do not speak in that manner, you had much better not speak at all. All the learning you have, or ever can have, is not worth one groat without it. It may be a comfort, and an amusement to you, in your closet, but can be of no use to you in the world. Let me conjure you, therefore, to make this your only object, till you have absolutely conquered it, for that is in your power; think of nothing else, read and speak for nothing else. Read aloud, though alone, and read articulately and distinctly, as if you were reading in public, and on the most important occasion. Recite pieces of eloquence, declaim scenes of tragedies, to some confidant, as if he were a numerous audience. If there is any particular consonant which you have a difficulty in articulating, utter it millions and millions of times, till you have uttered it right. Never speak quick, till you have first learned to speak well. In short, lay aside every book and every thought, that does not directly tend to this great object, absolutely decisive of your future fortune and figure.

You must be a good speaker. I use the word *must*, because I know you may, if you will. The vulgar, who are always mistaken, look upon a speaker and a comet, with the same astonishment and admiration; taking them both for præternatural phænomena. This error discourages many young men from attempting that character; and good speakers are willing to have their talent considered as something very extraordinary, if not a peculiar gift of God, to his elect. But let you and me analyze and simplify this good speaker: let us strip him of those adventitious plumes, with which his own pride, and the ignorance

of others, have decked him; and we shall find
the true definition of him to be no more than
this—A man of good common sense, who reasons justly, and expresses himself elegantly,
on that subject upon which he speaks. There
is, surely, no witchcraft in this. A man of
sense, without a superior and astonishing degree of parts, will not talk nonsense, upon any
subject; nor will he, if he has the least taste
or application, talk inelegantly. To what,
then, does all this mighty art and mystery of
speaking in Parliament amount? Why, no
more than this: that the man who speaks in
the House of Commons, speaks in that house,
and to four hundred people, that opinion, upon
a given subject, which he would make no difficulty of speaking in any house in England,
round the fire, or at table, to any fourteen people whatsoever—better judges, perhaps, and
severer critics of what he says, than any fourteen gentlemen of the House of Commons.

I have spoken frequently in Parliament, and
not always without some applause; and, therefore, I can assure you from my experience,
that there is very little in it. The elegancy
of the style, and the turn of the periods, make
the chief impression upon the hearers. Give
them but one or two round and harmonious
periods, in a speech, which they will retain
and repeat, and they will go home as well satisfied as people do from an opera, humming
all the way one or two favourite tunes that
have struck their ears and were easily caught.
Most people have ears, but few have judgment;
tickle those ears, and, depend upon it, you will
catch their judgments, such as they are.

Cicero, in his book *De Oratore*, in order to

raise the dignity of that profession, of which
he well knew himself to be at the head, asserts, that a complete orator must be a complete every thing—lawyer, philosopher, divine, &c. That would be extremely well, if it
were possible; but man's life is not long
enough; and I hold him to be the completest
orator, who speaks the best upon that subject
which occurs; whose happy choice of words,
whose lively imagination, whose elocution and
action, adorn and grace his matter; at the
same time that they excite the attention, and
engage the passions of his audience.

It is a very true saying, that a man must
be born a poet, but that he can make himself
an orator; and the very first principle of an
orator is, to speak his own language particularly, with the utmost purity and elegance.
A man will be forgiven, even great errors,
in a foreign language; but in his own, even
the least slips are justly laid hold of, and ridiculed.

I repeat it—it is certain, that, by study and
application, every man can make himself a
pretty good orator—eloquence depending upon
observation and care. Every man, if he
pleases, may choose good words, instead of
bad ones, may speak properly instead of improperly, may be clear and perspicuous in his
recitals, instead of dark and muddy; he may
have grace, instead of awkwardness, in his
motions and gestures; and, in short, may be a
very agreeable, instead of a very disagreeable
speaker, if he will take care and pains; and
surely it is very well worth while to take a
great deal of pains, to excel other men in that
particular article, in which they excel beasts.

If you imagine that speaking plain and una-dorned sense and reason, will do your business, you will find yourself most grossly mistaken. As a speaker, you will be ranked only accord-ing to your eloquence, and by no means ac-cording to your matter; every body knows the matter almost alike, but few can adorn it. It is by no means sufficient to be free from faults, in speaking and writing; you must do both correctly and elegantly. In faults of this kind, it is not *ille optimus qui minimis urge-tur.** But he is unpardonable who has any at all, because it is his own fault. He needs only attend to, observe, and imitate the best authors.

Constant experience has shown me, that great purity and elegance of style, with a graceful elocution, cover a multitude of faults, in either a speaker or a writer. For my own part, I confess (and I believe most people are of my mind) that, if a speaker should ungrace-fully mutter and stammer out to me the sense of an angel, deformed by barbarisms and sole-cisms, or larded with vulgarisms, he should never speak to me a second time, if I could help it.

The next thing you should attend to, is, to speak whatever language you do speak, in its greatest purity, and according to the rules of grammar; for we must never offend against grammar, nor make use of words which are not really words. This is not all; for not to speak ill, is not sufficient; we must speak well; and the best method of attaining that is, to read the best authors with attention; and to

---

* He is the best, who has the fewest faults.

observe how people of fashion speak, and those who express themselves best; for working mechanics, common people, footmen, and maid servants, all speak ill. They make use of low and vulgar expressions, which people of rank never use.—In numbers, they join a singular noun to a plural verb; in genders, they confound masculine with feminine; and, in tenses, they often take one for another. In order to avoid all these faults, we must read with care, observe the turn and expressions of the best authors, and not pass a word that we do not understand, or concerning which we have the least doubt, without exactly inquiring its meaning.

Think of your words, and of their arrangement, before you speak; choose the most elegant, and place them in the best order. Consult your own ear, to avoid cacophony; and, what is very nearly as bad, monotony. Think also of your gesture and looks, when you are speaking even upon the most trifling subjects. The same things differently expressed, looked, and delivered, cease to be the same.

Style is the dress of thoughts; and let them be ever so just, if your style be homely, coarse, and vulgar, they will appear to as much disadvantage, and be as ill received, as would your person, though ever so well proportioned, if dressed in rags, dirt, and tatters. It is not every understanding that can judge of matter; but every ear can and does judge, more or less, of style: and were I either to speak or write to the public, I should prefer moderate matter, adorned with all the beauties and elegancies of style, to the strongest matter in the world, ill worded, and ill delivered.

In speaking, do not suffer yourself to be dazzled by false brilliancy, by unnatural expressions, nor by those antitheses so much in fashion. As a protection against such innovations, have recourse to your own good sense, and to the ancient authors. On the other hand, do not laugh at those who adopt such errors; you are as yet too young to act the critic, or to stand forth a severe avenger of the violated rights of good sense. Content yourself with not being perverted, but do not think of converting others; let them quietly enjoy their errors, in taste as well as in religion.

There is no subject, that may not properly, and which ought not to be adorned, by a certain elegancy and beauty of style. What can be more adorned, than Cicero's philosophical works? What more than Plato's? It is their eloquence, only, that has preserved and transmitted them down to us, through so many centuries; for their philosophy is wretched, and the reasoning miserable. But eloquence will always please, and has always pleased. Study it therefore; make it the object of your thoughts and attention. Use yourself to relate elegantly; that is a good step towards speaking well in Parliament. Take some political subject, turn it in your thoughts, consider what may be said, both for and against it, then put those arguments into writing, in the most correct and elegant English you can.

All these engaging and endearing accomplishments are mechanical, and to be acquired by care and observation, as easily as turning, or any other mechanical trade.

Sense and argument, though coarsely delivered, will have their weight in a private conversation, with two or three people of sense; but, in a public assembly, they will have none, if naked, and destitute of the advantages I have mentioned. Cardinal de Retz observes, very justly, that every numerous assembly, is a mob influenced by their passions, humours, and affections, which nothing but eloquence ever did, or ever can engage. Mind your diction, in whatever language you either write or speak; contract a habit of correctness and elegance; consider your style, even in the freest conversation, and most familiar letters. After, at least, if not before you have said a thing, reflect if you could not have said it better. Where you doubt of the propriety or elegance of a word or phrase, consult some good dead or living authority in that language. Use yourself to translate, from various languages, into English: correct those translations, till they satisfy your ear, as well as your understanding; and be convinced of this truth, That the best sense and reason in the world, will be as unwelcome in a public assembly, without these ornaments, as they will in public companies, without the assistance of manners and politeness.

Even letters of business will not only admit of certain graces, but be the better for them: but then, they must be scattered with a sparing and a skilful hand; they must fit their place exactly. They must decently adorn, without incumbering; and modestly shine, without glaring. But as this is the utmost degree of perfection in letters of business, I would not advise you to attempt those embellishments, till you have first carefully laid your foundation.

Now, if it be necessary to attend so particularly to our manner of speaking, it is much more so, with respect to the matter. Fine turns of expression, a genteel and correct style, are ornaments as requisite to common sense, as polite behaviour and an elegant address are to common good manners. They are great assistants in the point of pleasing. A gentleman, it is true, may be known in the meanest garb; but it admits not of a doubt, that he would be better received into good company, genteely and fashionably dressed, than if he were to appear in dirt and tatters.

In order to speak grammatically, and to express yourself pleasingly, I would recommend that you frequently translate any language with which you are acquainted, into English, and correct such translation, till the words, their order, and the periods, are agreeable to your own ear.

Vulgarism in language is another distinguishing mark of bad company and education. Expressions may be correct in themselves, and yet be vulgar, owing to their not being fashionable: for language and manners are both established by the usage of people of fashion.

Orthography, in the true sense of the word, is so absolutely necessary for a man of letters, or a gentleman, that one false spelling may fix a ridicule upon him for the rest of his life; and I know a man of quality who never recovered the ridicule of having spelled *wholesome* without the *w*.

Reading with care will secure every body from false spelling; for books are always well spelled, according to the orthography of the times. Some words are indeed doubtful, being spelled differently, by different authors, of equal authority: but those are few; and in those cases every man has his option, because he may plead his authority either way: but, where there is but one right way, as in the two words abovementioned, it is unpardonable, and ridiculous, for a gentleman to miss it: even a woman of a tolerable education would despise, and laugh at a lover, who should send her an ill-spelled *billet-doux*. I fear, and suspect, that you have taken it into your head, in most cases, that the matter is all, and the manner little or nothing. If you have, undeceive yourself, and be convinced, that in every thing, the manner is fully as important as the matter. If you write epistles as well as Cicero, but in a very bad hand, and very ill-spelled, whoever receives, will laugh at them; and if you had the figure of an Adonis, with an awkward air and motions, it will disgust instead of pleasing.

The conversation of a low bred man, is filled up with proverbs and hackneyed sayings. Instead of observing that tastes are different, and that most men have one peculiar to themselves, he will give you, " What is one man's meat is another man's poison;" or, " Every one to their liking, as the old woman said, when she kissed her cow." He has ever some favourite word, which he introduces upon all occasions, right or wrong; such as, *vastly* angry, *vastly* kind; *devilish* ugly, *devilish* handsome; *immensely* great, *immensely little*. Even his pronunciation carries the mark of vulgarity along with it: he calls the earth, *yearth;* finan'ces, *fin'ances;* inqui'ry, *en'quirry;* he

goes *to wards* and not towards such a place.
He affects to use hard words, to give him the
appearance of a man of learning, but frequently mistakes their meaning, and seldom, if ever,
pronounces them properly.

All this must be avoided, if you would not
be supposed to have kept company with footmen and housemaids. Never have recourse to
proverbial or vulgar sayings; use neither favourite nor hard words, but seek for the most
elegant; be careful in the management of
them, and depend on it your labour will not be
lost; for nothing is more engaging, than a
fashionable and polite address.

There is a certain distinguishing diction,
that marks the man of fashion, a certain language of conversation, of which every gentleman should be master. Saying to a man just
married, "I wish you joy," or to one who has
lost his wife, "I am sorry for your loss," and
both perhaps with an unmeaning countenance.
may be civil, but it is nevertheless vulgar. A
man of fashion will express the same thing
more elegantly, and with a look of sincerity,
that shall attract the esteem of the person to
whom he speaks. He will advance to the one,
with warmth and cheerfulness, and perhaps
squeezing him by the hand, will say, "Believe
me, my dear Sir, I have scarcely words to express the joy I feel, upon your happy alliance
with such or such a family," &c. To the
other, in affliction, he will advance slower, and
with a peculiar composure of voice and countenance, begin his compliments of condolence
with, "I hope, Sir, you will do me the justice
to be persuaded that I am not insensible of
your unhappiness, that I take part in your dis-

:ress, and shall ever be affected when *you* are so."

Attention will do all this; and without attention, nothing is to be done. Want of attention, which is really want of thought, is either folly or madness. You should not only have attention to every thing, but a quickness of attention, so as to observe, at once, all the people in the room, their motions, their looks, and their words; and yet without staring at them, and seeming to be an observer. This quick and unobserved observation, is of infinite advantage in life, and is to be acquired with care; and, on the contrary, what is called absence, which is a thoughtlessness, and want of attention about what is doing, makes a man so like either a fool or a madman, that, for my part, I see no real difference. A fool never has thought; a madman has lost it; and an absent man is, for the time, without it.

INDOLENCE.

But why am I so particular, in pressing so many things upon your attention? Upon no other supposition, surely, than continued exertion until the end shall have been gained. I can hardly suppose you uncommonly indolent. But that you may shake off this state of inactivity—so natural, in a certain degree, to the human mind—I must crave your attention to it, as to other things that obstruct the progress of youth.

If I did not know, by experience, that some men pass their whole time in doing nothing,

I should not think it possible for any being, superior to Monsieur Descarte's automatons, to squander away, in absolute idleness, one single minute of that small portion of time which is allotted to us in this world.

There are two sorts of understandings; one of which hinders a man from ever being considerable, and the other commonly makes him ridiculous;—I mean the lazy mind, and the trifling frivolous mind. Yours, I hope, is neither. The lazy mind will not take the trouble of going to the bottom of any thing; but, discouraged by the first difficulties (and every thing worth knowing or having is attended with some) stops short, contents itself with easy, and consequently, superficial knowledge, and prefers a great degree of ignorance, to a small degree of trouble. These people either think, or represent, most things as impossible; whereas few things are so, to industry and activity. But difficulties seem to them impossibilities, or at least they pretend to think them so, by way of excuse for their laziness. An hour's attention, to the same object, is too laborious for them: they take every thing in the light in which it first presents itself, never consider it in all its different views; and, in short, never think it through. The consequence of this is, that when they come to speak upon these subjects, before people who have considered them with attention, they only discover their own ignorance and laziness, and lay themselves open to answers that put them in confusion. Do not, then, be discouraged, by the first difficulties, but *contra audentior ito;*.and resolve to go to the bottom of

* Be, on the contrary, more determined.

all those things, which every gentleman ought to know well. Those arts or sciences, which are peculiar to certain professions, need not be deeply known by those who are not intend- ed for those professions. As for instance, for- tification and navigation; of both which, a su- perficial and general knowledge, such as the common course of conversation, with a very little inquiry on your part, will give you, is sufficient.

Laziness of mind, or inattention, is as great an enemy to knowledge, as incapacity; for, in truth, what difference is there between a man who will not, and a man who cannot be in- formed? This difference only, that the former is justly to be blamed, the latter to be pitied. Yet, how many are there, very capable of re- ceiving knowledge, who, from laziness, inat- tention, and incuriousness, will not so much as ask for it, much less take the least pains to acquire it?

Your laziness, if you indulge it, will make you stagnate in a contemptible obscurity all your life. It will hinder you from doing any thing that will deserve to be written, or from writing any thing that may deserve to be read; and yet one or other of these two ob- jects, should be at least aimed at, by every ra- tional being. I look upon indolence as a sort of suicide; for the man is effectually destroy- ed by it, though the appetites of the brute may survive. Use yourself, therefore, in time, to be alert and diligent, in your little concerns.. Never procrastinate, never put off till to-mor- row, what you can do to-day; and never do two things at a time: pursue your object, be it what it will, steadily and indefatigably; and let any

difficulties (if surmountable) rather animate
than slacken your endeavours. Perseverance
has surprising effects.

Examine carefully, and reconsider all your
notions of things; analyse them, and discover
their component parts; and see if habit and
prejudice are not the principal. Weigh the
matter upon which you are to form your opinion, in the equal and impartial scales of reason. It is not to be conceived how many people, capable of reasoning, if they would, live
and die in a thousand errors, from laziness:
they will rather adopt the prejudices of others,
than give themselves the trouble of forming
opinions of their own. They say things, at
first, because other people have said them;
and then 'they persist in them, because they
have said them themselves.

Sloth, indolence, and *mollesse*,* are pernicious, and unbecoming a young man; let them
be your *ressource* forty years hence, at soonest. Determine, at all events, and however
disagreeable it may be to you, in some respects, and for some time, to keep the most
distinguished and fashionable company of the
place you are at, either for their rank, or for
their learning. This gives you credentials to
the best companies, wherever you go afterwards. Pray, therefore, no indolence, no laziness; but employ every minute of your life in
active pleasures or useful employments.

The ignorant and the weak, only, are idle;
but those who have once acquired a good
stock of knowledge, always desire to increase
it. Knowledge is like power, in this respect,

* Effeminacy.

that those who have the most, are most desirous of having more. It does not clog by possession, but increases desire; which is the case of very few pleasures.

Believe me, there is scarcely one person without some alloy of indolence. Thousands spend more time in an idle uncertainty, as to *which* to begin *first*, of two affairs, than would have been sufficient to have ended them both. The occasion of this seems to be, the want of some necessary employment, to put the spirits in motion, and awaken them out of their lethargy. Were one's time a little straitened in business, like water enclosed in banks, it would have some determined course; but otherwise it becomes a deluge, without either rise or motion.

You may rest assured, it will require all your resolution to guard against the inroads of indolence. I can stifle any violent inclination, or oppose a torrent of anger, with more success. Indolence is a stream which flows slowly on, but yet undermines the foundation of every virtue. It is a rust of the mind, more to be dreaded than even a more lively vice, as it lends a tincture of itself to every action of life.

OBSERVATION.

As the art of pleasing is to be learnt only by frequenting the best companies, we must endeavour to pick it up in such companies, by observation. It is not sense and knowledge, alone, that will acquire esteem; these certainly are the first and necessary foundations for pleasing; but they will by no means attain it, unless attended with manners and attention.

There have been people who have frequented the first companies all their life time, and yet have never divested themselves of their natural stiffness and awkwardness; but have continued as vulgar as if they were never out of a servant's hall. This has been owing to carelessness, and a want of attention to the manners and behaviour of others.

There are a great many people, likewise, who busy themselves the whole day, and who in fact do nothing. They have possibly taken up a book, for two or three hours; but, from a certain inattention, that grows upon them, the more it is indulged, know no more of the contents, than if they had not looked into it. It is impossible for any one to retain what he reads, unless he reflects and reasons upon it as he proceeds. When they have thus lounged away an hour or two, they will saunter into company, without attending to any thing that passes there; but, if they think at all, are thinking of some trifling matter, that ought not to occupy their attention. Thence, perhaps they go to the play; where they stare at the company and the lights, without attending to the piece—the very thing they went to see. In this manner, they wear away their hours, that might otherwise be employed to their improvement and advantage. This silly suspension of thought, they would pass for *absence of mind.*—Ridiculous! Wherever you are, let me recommend it to you to pay an attention to all that passes; observe the characters of the persons you are with, and the subjects of their conversation; listen to every thing that is said, see every thing that is done.

A man is fit for neither business nor pleasure, who either cannot, or does not, command and direct his attention to the present object; and, in some degree, banish, for that time, all other objects from his thoughts. If, at a party of pleasure, a man were to be solving, in his own mind, a problem in Euclid, he would be a very bad companion, and make a very poor figure in that company; or if, in studying a problem in his closet, he were to think of a minuet, I am apt to believe that he would make a very poor mathematician. There is time enough for every thing, in the course of the day, if you do but one thing at once; but there is not time enough in the year, if you will do two things at a time. The pensionary De Witt, who was torn to pieces in the year 1672, did the whole business of the republic; and yet had time left to go to assemblies in the evening, and sup in company. Being asked, How he could possibly find time to go through so much business, and yet amuse himself in the evenings, as he did: he answered, There was nothing so easy: it was only doing one thing at a time, and never putting off any thing, till to-morrow, that could be done to-day. This steady and undissipated attention, to one object, is a sure mark of a superior genius; as hurry, bustle, and agitation, are the never failing symptoms of a weak and frivolous mind.

Hoc age, was a maxim among the Romans; which means, Do what you are about, and do that only. A little mind is hurried by twenty things at once; but a man of sense does but

one thing at a time, and resolves to excel in
it; for whatever is worth doing at all, is worth
doing well. Therefore, remember to give
yourself up entirely to the thing you are doing, be it what it may, whether your book or
your play; for if you have a right ambition,
you will desire to excel all boys of your age.
at cricket, at trap-ball, as well as in learning
I advise you thus, because I would by no
means have any thing, that is known to others.
be totally unknown to you. It is a great advantage for any man to be able to talk, or to hear,
neither ignorantly nor absurdly, upon any subject; for I have known people, who have not
said one word, hear ignorantly and absurdly:
it has appeared in their inattentive and unmeaning faces.

Without attention, it is impossible to remember; and without remembering, it is but
time and labour lost, to learn. I hope, too,
that your attention is not employed merely
upon words, but upon the sense and meaning
of those words; that is, that when you read, or
get any thing by heart, you observe the
thoughts and reflections of the author, as well
as his words.

A continual inattention to matters that occur, is the characteristic of a weak mind. The
man who habituates himself to it, is little else
than a trifler, a blank in society, which every
sensible person overlooks. Surely, what is
worth doing, is worth doing well; and nothing
can be well done, without proper attention.
When I hear a man say, on being asked about
any thing that was said or done in his presence,
"that truly he did not mind it," I am ready to
knock the fool down. *Why* did not he mind

it? What else had he to do? A man of sense and fashion never makes use of this paltry plea: he never complains of a treacherous memory, but attends to and remembers every thing that is either said or done.

Attend not only to what people say, but observe also how they say it; and, if you have any sagacity, you may discover more truth by your eyes, than by your ears. People can say what they will, but they cannot look just as they will; and their looks frequently discover what their words are calculated to conceal. Observe, therefore, people's looks carefully, when they speak, not only to you, but to each other. I have often guessed, by people's faces, what they were saying, though I could not hear one word they said. The most material knowledge of all, I mean the knowledge of the world, is never to be acquired without great attention; and I know many old people, who, though they have lived long in the world, are but children, still, as to the knowledge of it, from their levity and inattention. Certain forms, with which all people comply, and certain arts, at which all people aim, hide, in some degree, the truth, and give to almost every person, a general exterior resemblance. Attention and sagacity must see through that veil, and discover the natural character. You are of an age, now, to reflect, to observe and compare characters, and to arm yourself against the common arts, at least, of the world.

Whenever, then, you go into good company, that is, the company of people of fashion, observe carefully their behaviour, their address, and their manner. Imitate them, as far as in

E

your power. Your attention, if possible, should
be so ready, as to observe every person in the
room, at once, their motions, their looks, and
their turns of expression; and that without
staring or seeming to be an observer. This
kind of observation may be acquired, by care
and practice; and will be found of the utmost
advantage, in the course of life.

ABSENCE OF MIND.

HAVING mentioned absence of mind, let me
be more particular concerning it.

What the world calls an absent man, is generally either a very affected, or a very weak
man; but, whether weak, or affected, he is, in
company, a very disagreeable man. Lost in
thought, or possibly in no thought at all, he is
a stranger to every one present, and to every
thing that passes; he knows not his best
friends, is deficient in every act of good manners, unobservant of the actions of the company, and insensible to his own. His answers
are quite the reverse of what they ought to
be: talk to him of one thing, he replies as of
another. He forgets what he said last, leaves
his hat in one room, and his cane in another;
nay, if it were not for his buckles, he would
even leave his shoes behind him. Neither his
arms nor his legs, seem to be a part of his
body; and his head is never in a right position. He joins not in the general conversation, except it be by fits and starts, as if
awaking from a dream. I attribute this either
to weakness or affectation. His shallow mind

is possibly not able to attend to more than one
thing at a time; or he would be supposed
wrapt up in the investigation of some very important matter. Such men as Sir Isaac Newton, or Mr. Locke, might occasionally have
some excuse for absence of mind: it might
proceed from that intenseness of thought, that
was necessary, at all times, for the scientific
subjects they were studying; but, for a young
man, and a man of the world, who has no such
plea to make, absence of mind is a rudeness to
the company, and deserves the severest censure.

But that you may be thoroughly cured of
absence, I shall here insert the portrait of an
Absent Man, from Bruyere.

"Menalcas," says that excellent author,
"comes down in a morning, opens his door to
go out, but shuts it again, because he per-
ceives that he has his night-cap on; and examining himself further, finds that he is but
half shaved, that he has stuck his sword on his
right side, that his stockings are about his
heels, and that his shirt is over his breeches.
When he is dressed, he goes to court, comes
into the drawing-room, and walking bolt-up-
right under a branch of candlesticks, his wig
is caught up by one of them, and hangs dang-
ling in the air. All the courtiers fall a laughing, but Menalcas laughs louder than any of
them, and looks about for the person that is
the jest of the company. Coming down to
the court-gate he finds a coach, which taking
for his own, he whips into it; and the coach-
man drives off, not doubting but he carries his
master. As soon as he stops, Menalcas throws
himself out of the coach, crosses the court,

ascends the stair-case, and runs through all
the chambers with the greatest familiarity;
reposes himself on a couch, and fancies himself at home. The master of the house at
last comes in; Menalcas rises to receive him,
and desires him to sit down; he talks, muses,
and then talks again. The gentleman of the
house is tired and amazed; Menalcas is no less
so, but is every moment in hopes that his impertinent guest will at last end his tedious
visit. Night comes on, when Menalcas is
hardly undeceived.

" When he is playing at backgammon, he
calls for a full glass of wine and water; it is
his turn to throw, he has the box in one hand,
and his glass in the other; and being extremely dry, and unwilling to lose time, he swallows
down both the dice, and at the same time
throws his wine into the tables. He writes a
letter, and flings the sand into the ink-bottle;
he writes a second, and mistakes the super-
scription. A nobleman receives one of them,
and upon opening it reads as follows: ' I would
have you, honest Jack, immediately upon the
receipt of this, take in hay enough to serve
me the winter.' His farmer receives the
other, and is amazed to see in it, ' My lord, I
received your grace's commands, with an en-
tire submission to—.' If he is at an entertainment, you may see the pieces of bread continually multiplying round his plate. It is
true, the rest of the company want it, as well
as their knives and forks, which Menalcas does
not let them keep long. Sometimes in a morning he puts his whole family in a hurry, and at
last goes out without being able to stay for his
coach or dinner, and for that day you may see

him in every part of the town, except the very place where he had appointed to be upon a business of importance. You would often take him for every thing that he is not; for a fellow quite stupid, for he hears nothing; for a fool, for he talks to himself, and has an hundred grimaces and motions with his head, which are altogether involuntary; for a proud man, for he looks full upon you, and takes no notice of your saluting him. The truth of it is, his eyes are open, but he makes no use of them, and neither sees you, nor any man, nor any thing else. He came once from his country-house, and his own footman undertook to rob him, and succeeded. They held a flambeau to his throat, and bid him deliver his purse; he did so, and coming home told his friends he had been robbed; they desired to know the particulars, ' Ask my servants,' says Menalcas, ' for they were with me.' "

However insignificant a company may be; however trifling their conversation; while you are with them, do not show them, by any inattention, that you think them trifling; that can never be the way to please; but rather fall in with their weakness than otherwise; •for to mortify or show the least contempt to those with whom we are in company, is the greatest rudeness we can be guilty of, and what few can forgive.

I know no one thing more offensive to a company, than inattention and distraction. It is showing them the utmost contempt; and people never forgive contempt. No man is *distrait*,* with the man he fears, or with the

---

* Absent.

woman he loves; which is a proof that every
man can get the better of that distraction,
when he thinks it worth his while to do so;
and, take my word for it, it is always worth his
while. For my own part, I would rather be
in company with a dead man, than with an absent one; for if the dead man gives me no
pleasure, at least he shows me no contempt;
whereas, the absent man, silently indeed, but
very plainly, tells me that he does not think
me worth his attention. Besides, can an absent man make any observations upon the characters, customs, and manners of the company?
No. He may be in the best companies all his
life-time (if they will admit him, which, if I
were they, I would not) and never be one jot
the wiser. I never will converse with an absent man; one may as well talk to a deaf one.
It is, in truth, a practical blunder, to address
ourselves to a man, who, we see plainly, neither hears, minds, nor understands us. Moreover, I aver that no man is, in any degree, fit
for either business or conversation, who cannot, and does not, direct and command his attention to the present object, be that what it
will. .

An absent man can make but few observations; and those will be disjointed and imperfect, as half the circumstances must necessarily escape him. He can pursue nothing steadily; because his absence makes him lose his
way. They are very disagreeable, and hardly
to be tolerated, in old age; but, in youth, they
cannot be forgiven. If you find that you have
the least tendency to them, pray watch yourself very carefully, and you may prevent them
now; but if you let them grow into a habit,

you will find it very difficult to cure them, hereafter; and a worse distemper I do not know.

If, therefore, you would rather please, than offend; rather be well, than ill spoken of; rather be loved, than hated; remember to have that constant attention about you, which flatters every man's little vanity; and the want of which, by mortifying his pride, never fails to excite his resentment, or at least his ill-will.

FRIENDSHIP.

Tully was the first who observed, that friendship improves happiness, and abates misery, by doubling joy, and dividing grief. It is a just thought. But our chief difficulty is, to ascertain what friendship really is; and upon what principles it ought to be formed. It has been so often and so finely painted, as to fall in the way of every reader; but the misery is, it is generally painted in flattering colours; at least the evils of what is commonly called friendship, are not sketched with a faithful hand.

The season of youth, is the season of attachments. The heart is then susceptible of the finest impressions, and is too little concerned about the objects of its attachments, or the circumstances in which they ought to be formed. This makes counsel the more necessary; and who so likely to give it well, as those who have had experience?

By friendship, I do not mean that refined and almost supernatural attachment, which is to be found in the poets; of which, there have not, perhaps, been three instances, since the creation; but only that ordinary friendship, which is so much talked of, and, such as it is, has some existence; a friendship which consists in speaking well of one, and prompts those who have it, to acts of kindness, rather than injury, consistently with their own interest.

People of your age, have commonly an unguarded frankness about them; which makes them the easy prey and bubbles of the artful and the experienced. They look upon every knave, or fool, who tells them that he is their friend, to be really so; and pay that profession of simulated friendship, with an indiscreet and unbounded confidence, always to their loss, often to their ruin. Beware, therefore, now that you are coming into the world, of these proffered friendships. Receive them with civility, but with great incredulity, too; and pay them with civility, but not with confidence. Do not let your vanity and self-love, make you suppose that people become your friends at first sight, or even upon a short acquaintance. Real friendship is a slow grower; and never thrives, unless ingrafted upon a stock of known and reciprocal merit. There is another kind of nominal friendship, among young people, which is warm for the time, but, by good luck, of short duration. This friendship is hastily produced, by their being accidentally thrown together, and pursuing the same course of riot and debauchery. A fine friendship truly! and well cemented by drunkenness and lewdness. It should rather be called a conspiracy against morals and good manners, and be punished as such by the civil magistrate. However, they have the impudence, and the folly, to call this confederacy a friendship. They lend one another money, for bad purposes; they engage in quarrels, offensive and defensive, for their accomplices; they tell one another all they know, and often more, too; when, on a sudden, some accident disperses them, and they think no more of each other, unless it be to betray, and laugh at their imprudent confidence. Remember to make a great difference between companions and friends; for a very complaisant and agreeable companion may, and often does, prove a very improper, and a very dangerous friend. People will, in a great degree, and not without reason, form their opinion of you, upon that which they have of your friends; and there is a Spanish proverb, which says, very justly, *Tell me with whom you live, and I will tell you who you are.* One may fairly suppose, that a man, who chooses a knave or a fool for his friend, has something very bad to do, or to conceal. But, at the same time that you carefully decline the friendship of knaves and fools, if it can be called friendship, there is no occasion to make either of them your enemies, wantonly, and unprovoked: they are numerous bodies; and I would choose rather a secure neutrality, than alliance, or war, with either of them. You may be a declared enemy to their vices and follies, without being marked out by them as a personal one. Their enmity is the next dangerous thing to their friendship. Have a real reserve with almost every body; and have a seeming reserve with almost nobody; for it is very disagreeable to seem reserved, and

E 2

very dangerous not to be so. Few people find the true medium; many are ridiculously mysterious and reserved, upon trifles; and many imprudently communicate all they know.

Be cautious, therefore, how you contract friendships; but be desirous, and even industrious, to obtain a universal acquaintance. Be easy, and even forward, in making new acquaintances; that is the only way of knowing manners and characters in general.

Be one, if you will, in young companies, and bear your part, like others, in all the social festivity of youth; nay, trust them with your innocent frolics, but keep your serious matters to yourself. If you must, at any time, make *them* known, let it be to some tried friend, of great experience; and, that nothing may tempt him to become your rival, let that friend be in a different walk of life from yourself; for I would not advise you to depend so much upon the heroic virtue of mankind, as to hope, or believe, that your competitor will ever be your friend, as to the object of that competition.

In contracting your friendships, single out those who possess a certain evenness of temper. There are some persons who are, at certain periods, inexpressibly agreeable, and at others detestable and odious. It is very unfortunate to be entangled in a friendship, with one of this character.

In a word, as you wish to possess in yourself virtue, knowledge, discretion, fidelity and honour, seek such as have most of these qualities, and to them confine your friendships.

KNOWLEDGE OF THE WORLD.

A KNOWLEDGE OF THE WORLD, by our own experience and observation, is so necessary, that, without it, we shall act very absurdly, and frequently give offence, when we do not mean it. All the learning and parts in the world, will not secure us from it. Without an acquaintance with life, a man may say very good things, but time them so ill, and address them so improperly, that he had much better be silent. Full of himself and his own business, and inattentive to the circumstances and situations of those with whom he converses, he vents it, without the least discretion, says things that he ought not to say, confuses some, shocks others, and puts the whole company in pain, lest what he utters next should prove worse than the last. The best direction I can give you, in this matter, is, rather to fall in with the conversation of others, than start a subject of your own; rather strive to put them more in conceit with themselves, than to draw their attention to you.

Man is made up of such a variety of matter, that, to search him thoroughly, requires time and attention. Though we are all made of the same materials, and have all the same passions, yet, from a difference in their proportion and combination, we vary in our dispositions. What is agreeable to one, is disagreeable to another. Reason is given us to control those passions, but seldom does it. Application, therefore, to the reason of any man, will frequently prove ineffectual, unless we endeavour, at the same time, to gain his heart.

A man requires very little knowledge and experience of the world, to understand glaring, high-coloured, and decided characters. They are but few, and they strike at first. But to distinguish the almost imperceptible shades, and the nice gradations of virtue and vice, sense and folly, strength and weakness, (of which, characters are commonly composed) demands some experience, great observation, and minute attention. In the same cases, most people do the same things; but, with this material difference, upon which the success commonly turns—A man who has studied the world, knows when to time, and where to place them; he has analyzed the characters to whom he applies, and adapted his address and his arguments to them: but a man of what is called plain good sense, who has reasoned only by himself, and not acted with mankind, mistimes, misplaces, runs precipitately and bluntly at the mark, and falls upon his nose in the way. In the common manners of social life, every man of common sense has the rudiments, the A B C of civility: he means not to offend, and even wishes to please; and if he has any real merit, will be received and tolerated in good company. But that is far from being enough. Though he may be received, he will never be desired; though he does not offend, he will never be loved; but like some little, insignificant, neutral power, surrounded by great ones, he will neither be feared nor courted by any; but, by turns, invaded by all, whenever it is their interest. A most contemptible situation! Whereas, a man who has carefully attended to the various workings of the heart, and the artifices of the head, and has experienced them; and who, by one shade, can trace the progression of the whole colour; who can, at the proper times, employ all the several means of persuading the understanding, and engaging the heart; may, and will have enemies, but will and must have friends: he may be opposed, but he will also be supported; his talents may excite the jealousy of some, but his engaging manners will make him beloved by many more; he will be considerable, he will be considered. Many different qualifications must conspire, to form such a man, and to make him at once respectable and amiable; and the least must be joined to the greatest. The latter would be unavailing, without the former; and the former would be futile and frivolous, without the latter. Learning is acquired by reading books; but the much more necessary learning—the knowledge of the world—is to be acquired only by reading men, and studying all their various editions. Many words, in every language, are generally thought to be synonymous; but those who study the language attentively, will find that there is no such thing; they will discover some little difference, some distinction, between all those words that are vulgarly called synonymous. One has always more energy, extent, or delicacy, than another: it is the same with men; all are in general, and yet no two, in particular, exactly alike. Those who have not actually studied, perpetually mistake them. They do not discern the shades and gradations that distinguish characters seemingly alike. Company, various company, is the only school for this knowledge.

Young people are very apt to overrate both

men and things, from not being enough acquainted with them. In proportion as you
come to know them better, you will value
them less. You will find that reason, which
always ought to direct mankind, seldom does;
but that passions and weaknesses commonly
usurp its seat, and rule in its stead.

To know mankind well, requires fully as
much attention and application, as to know
books; and, perhaps, more sagacity and discernment. I am, at this time, acquainted with
many elderly people, who have all passed their
whole lives in the great world, but with such
levity and inattention, that they know no
more of it now, than they did at fifteen. Do
not flatter yourself, therefore, with the thoughts
that you can acquire this knowledge in the
frivolous chit-chat of idle companies. You
must go much deeper than that. You must
look *into* people as well as *at* them. Almost
all people are born with all the passions, to a
certain degree; but almost every man has a
prevailing passion, to which the others are
subordinate.

Wherever, then, you are, search into the
characters of men. Find out, if possible, their
foible, their governing passion, or their particular merit. Take them on their weak side,
and you will generally succeed; their prevailing vanity you may readily discover, by observing their favourite topic of conversation;
for every one talks most of that in which he
would be thought most to excel; and when
you have found out the prevailing passion of
any man, remember never to trust him, where
that passion is concerned.

In **order** to profit by your knowledge of men,

the time should also be judiciously chosen.
Every man has his particular times, when he
may be applied to with success; the *mollia
tempora fandi;** but these times are not all
day long; they must be found out, watched,
and taken advantage of. You could not hope
for success, in applying to a man about one
business, when he was taken up with another,
or when his mind was affected with excess of
grief, anger, or the like.

You cannot judge of other men's minds better, than by studying your own. Though one
man has one foible, and another has another,
yet men in general are very much alike.
Whatever pleases or offends you, will, in similar circumstances, please or offend others. If
you find yourself hurt, when another makes
you feel his superiority, you will certainly,
upon the common rule of right, *do as you
would be done by*, take care not to let another
feel *your* superiority, if you have it; especially
if you wish to gain his interest or esteem. If
disagreeable insinuations, open contradictions,
or oblique sneers, vex and anger you, would
you use them where you wished to please?
Certainly not. Observe, then, with care, the
operations of your own mind, and you may, in
a great measure, read all mankind.

A vulgar, ordinary way of thinking, acting,
or speaking, implies a low education, and a
habit of low company. Young people contract
it at school, or among servants, with whom
they are too often used to converse; but, after
they frequent good company, they must want
attention and observation very much, if they

---

* The favourable occasions for speaking.

do not lay it quite aside. Indeed, if they do not, good company will be very apt to lay them aside. The various kinds of vulgarisms are infinite. I cannot pretend to point them out; but I will give some samples, by which you may guess at the rest.

A vulgar man is captious and jealous: eager and impetuous, about trifles. He suspects himself to be slighted, thinks every thing that is said is meant at him: if the company happen to laugh, he is persuaded they laugh at him; he grows angry and testy, says something very impertinent, and draws himself into a scrape, by showing what he calls a proper spirit, and asserting himself. A man of fashion does not suppose himself to be either the sole or principal object of the thoughts, looks, or words of the company; and never suspects that he is either slighted or laughed at, unless he is conscious that he deserves it. If (which very seldom happens) the company is absurd or ill-bred enough to do either, he cares not, unless the insult be so gross and plain, as to require satisfaction of another kind. As he is above trifles, he is never vehement and eager about them; and, wherever they are concerned, rather acquiesces than wrangles.

Do not imagine that the knowledge, which I so much recommend to you, is confined to books; pleasing, useful, and necessary, as that knowledge is: but I comprehend in it the great knowledge of the world, still more necessary than that of books. In truth, they assist one another, reciprocally; and no man will have either perfectly, who has not both. The knowledge of the world is to be acquired

only in the world, and not in a closet. Books
alone will never teach it; but they will suggest many things to your observation, which
might otherwise escape you; and your own
observations upon mankind, when compared
with those which you will find in books, will
help you to fix the true point.

Read, in the morning, some of La Rochefou-
cault's maxims; consider them, examine them
well, and compare them with the real characters you meet with in the evening. Read La
Bruyere in the morning, and see in the evening, whether his pictures are like. Study the
heart and the mind of man, and begin with
your own. Meditation and reflection must
lay the foundation of that knowledge; but experience and practice must, and alone can,
complete it. Books, it is true, point out the
operations of the mind, the sentiments of the
heart, the influence of the passions; and so far
they are of previous use: but, without subsequent practice, experience, and observation,
they are as ineffectual, and would even lead
you into as many errors in fact, as a map, if
you were to take your notions of the towns
and provinces from their delineations in it. A
man would reap very little benefit by his travels, if he made them only in his closet upon a
map of the whole world.

I will allow, that one bred up in a cloister
or college, may reason well on the structure
of the human mind. He may investigate the
nature of man, and give a tolerable account of
his head, his heart, his passions, and his sentiments; but, at the same time, he may know
nothing of him: he has not lived with him,
and of course knows but little how those sen-

timents or those passions will work. He must
be ignorant of the various prejudices, propen-
sities, and antipathies, that always bias, and
frequently determine him. His knowledge is
acquired only from theory, which differs widely from practice; and, if he forms his judgment from that alone, he must be often de-
ceived; whereas, a man of the world, one who
collects his knowledge from his own experience and observation, is seldom wrong. He
is well acquainted with the operations of the
human mind; pries into the heart of man;
reads his words before they are uttered; sees
his actions before they are performed; knows
what will please, and what will displease, and
foresees the event of most things.

Labour, then, to acquire this intuitive knowledge; attend carefully to the address, the
arts, and manners, of those acquainted with
life, and endeavour to imitate them. Observe
the means taken by them, to gain the favour
and conciliate the affections of those with
whom they associate; pursue those means,
and you will soon gain the esteem of all that
know you.

How often have we seen men governed by
persons very much their inferiors in point of
understanding, and even without their knowing it? A proof that some men have more
worldly dexterity than others: they find out
the weak and unguarded part, make their attack there, and the man surrenders.

Now, from a knowledge of mankind, we
shall learn the advantage of two things;—the
command of our temper and of our countenance. A trifling, disagreeable incident, shall
perhaps anger one unacquainted with life, or

confound him with shame; shall make him
rave like a madman, or look like a fool; but a
man of the world will never understand what
he cannot or ought not to resent. If he should
chance to make a slip himself, he will stifle
his confusion, and turn it off with a jest; recovering it with coolness.

Many people have sense enough to keep
their own secrets; but from being unused to a
variety of company, have unfortunately such a
tell-tale countenance, as involuntarily de-
clares what they would wish to conceal. This
is a great unhappiness, and should, as soon as
possible, be corrected.

That coolness of mind and evenness of
countenance, which prevents a discovery of
our sentiments, by our words, our actions, or
our looks, are too necessary to pass unnoticed.
A man who cannot hear displeasing things,
without visible marks of anger or uneasiness;
or pleasing ones, without a sudden burst of
joy, a cheerful eye, or an expanded face, is at
the mercy of every knave; for either he will
designedly please or provoke you himself
to catch your unguarded looks, or will seize
the opportunity thus to read your very heart,
when any other shall do it. You may possibly
tell me, that this coolness must be natural; for,
if not, you can never acquire it. I will admit
the force of constitution; but people are very
apt to blame that, for many things they might
readily avoid. Care, with a little reflection,
will soon give you this mastery of your temper
and countenance. If you find yourself
subject to sudden starts of passion, determine
with yourself not to utter a single word, until
your reason has recovered itself; and resolve

to keep your countenance as unmoved as possible. As a man, who at a card-table, can preserve a serenity in his looks, under good or bad luck, has considerably the advantage of one who appears elated with success, or cast down with ill fortune, from our being able to read his cards in his face; so the man of the world, having to deal with one of those babbling countenances, will take care to profit by the circumstance, let the consequence to him with whom he deals, be as injurious as it may.

If fools should attempt, at any time, to be witty upon you, the best way is, not to know their witticisms are levelled at you, but to conceal any uneasiness it may give you; but should they be so plain that you cannot be thought ignorant of their meaning, I would recommend, rather than quarrel with the company, joining even in the same laugh against yourself; allow the jest to be a good one, and take it in seeming good humour. Never attempt to retaliate the same way, as that would imply you were hurt.

Wrangling and quarrelling, are characteristic of a weak mind. Be *you* always above it. Enter into no sharp contest, and pride yourself in showing, if possible, more civility to your antagonist, than to any other in the company: this will infallibly bring over all the laughers to your side, and the person with whom your are contending, will be very likely to confess you have behaved very handsomely throughout the whole affair.

Experience will also teach us, that though all men consist principally of the same materials, as I before took notice, yet from a difference in their proportion, no two men are uniformly the same. We differ from one another, and we often differ from ourselves; that is, we sometimes do things utterly inconsistent with the general tenor of our characters. The wisest man may occasionally do a weak thing; the most honest man, a wrong thing; the proudest man, a mean thing; and the worst of men will sometimes do a good thing. On this account, our study of mankind should not be general. We should take a frequent view of individuals, and, though we may, upon the whole, form a judgment of the man from his prevailing passion, or his general character, yet it will be prudent not to determine, until we have waited to see the operations of his subordinate appetites and humours.

For example; a man's general character may be that of strictly honest. I would not dispute it, because I would not be thought envious or malevolent; but I would not rely upon this general character, so as to entrust him with my fortune or life. Should this honest man, as is not uncommon, be my rival in power, interest, or love, he may possibly do things that, in other circumstances, he would abhor; and power, interest, and love, let me tell you, will often put honesty to the severest trial, and frequently overpower it. I would then ransack this honest man to the bottom, if I wished to trust him, and as I found him, would place my confidence accordingly.

One of the great compositions in our nature, is vanity, to which all men, more or less, give way. Most women have an intolerable share of it. No flattery, no adulation, is too gross for them. Those who flatter them most, please them best, and they are most in love

with him, who pretends to be most in love
with them; and the least slight or contempt
of them is never forgotten. It is, in some
measure, the same with men; they will sooner
pardon an injury, than an insult; and are more
hurt by contempt, than by ill usage. Though
all men do not boast of superior talents; though
they pretend not to the abilities of a Pope, a
Newton, or a Bolingbroke; every one pretends
to have common sense, and to discharge his
office in life with common decency: to arraign,
therefore, in any shape, his abilities or integrity, in the department he holds, is an insult
he will not readily forgive.

As I would not have you trust too implicitly
to a man, because the world gives him a good
character, so I must particularly caution you
against those who speak well of themselves.
In general, suspect those who boast of any
one virtue above all others, or affect to have
it; for they are commonly impostors. There
are exceptions, however, to this rule; for we
hear of prudes that have been chaste, bullies
that have been brave, and saints that have
been religious. Confide only where your own
observation shall direct you. Observe not
only what is said, but how it is said; and if
you have any penetration, you may find out
the truth, better by your eyes, than your ears;
in short, never take a character upon common
report, but inquire into it yourself; for common report, though it is right in general, may
be wrong in particulars.

Were I to hear a man making strong pro-
testations, and swearing to the truth of a
thing, that is in itself probable and very likely
to be, I should doubt his veracity; for when he

takes such pains to make me believe it, it cannot be with a good design.

There is a certain easiness or false modesty, in most young people, that makes them either unwilling or ashamed to refuse any thing that is asked of them. There is also an unguarded openness about them, that makes them the ready prey of the artful and designing. They are easily led away, by the feigned friendships of a knave or a fool, and too rashly place a confidence in them, that terminates in their loss, and frequently in their ruin. Beware, therefore, as I said before, of these proffered friendships. Repay them with compliments, but not with confidence. Never let your vanity make you suppose, that people become your friends upon a slight acquaintance; for good offices must be shown on both sides, to create a friendship: it will not thrive, unless its love be mutual; and it requires time to ripen it.

This knowlege is the true object of a gentleman's travelling, if he travel as he ought to do. By frequenting good company, in every country, he himself becomes of every country. He is no longer an Englishman, a Frenchman, or an Italian; but he is a European: he adopts, respectively, the best manners of every country; and is a Frenchman at Paris, an Italian at Rome, an Englishman at London.

Having said thus much of the passions and conduct of others, let me now put you a little on your guard as respects your own. There are many little points of conduct, which are necessary, in the course of the world, and which he who practises the earliest, will please the most, and rise the soonest. The spirits and vivacity of youth are apt to neglect them as useless, or reject them as troublesome. But subsequent knowledge, and experience of the world, remind us of their importance, commonly when it is too late. The principal of these things, is the mastery of one's temper, and that coolness of mind, and serenity of countenance, which hinders us from disclosing, by words, actions, or even looks, those passions or sentiments, by which we are inwardly moved or agitated; and the discovery of which gives cooler and abler people such infinite advantage over us, not only in great business. but in all the most common occurrences of life. A man who does not possess himself enough to hear disagreeable things, without visible marks of anger and change of countenance, or agreeable without sudden bursts of joy, and expansion of countenance, is at the mercy of every artful knave, or pert coxcomb: the former will provoke or please you by design, to catch unguarded words or looks; by which, he will easily decypher the secrets of your heart, of which you should keep the key yourself, and trust it with no man living. The latter will, by his absurdity, and without intending it, produce the same discoveries, of which other people will avail themselves. You will say, possibly, that this coolness must be constitutional, and consequently does not depend upon the will: and I will allow that constitution has some power over us; but I will maintain, too, that people very often, to excuse themselves, very unjustly accuse their constitutions. Care and reflection, if properly used, will prevail; and a man may as surely get a habit of letting his reason prevail over his constitution, as of letting, as most people do, the latter prevail over the former. If you find yourself subject to sudden starts of passion, or madness (for I see no difference between them, but in their duration) resolve within yourself, at least, never to speak one word, while you feel that emotion within you. Determine, too, to keep your countenance as unmoved and unembarrassed as possible; of which steadiness, you may acquire a habit, by constant attention. This is so necessary at some games, that a man who had not the command of his temper, and countenance, would infallibly be undone by those who had, even though they played fair; and in political business, you always play with sharpers, to whom, at least, you should give no fair advantages.

If you find that you have a hastiness in your temper, which unguardedly breaks out into indiscreet sallies, or rough expressions, to either your superiors, your equals, or your inferiors, watch it narrowly, check it carefully, and call the *suavitèr in modo** to your assistance; at the first impulse of passion, be silent, till you can be soft. Labour even to get the command of your countenance, so well, that those emotions may not be read in it;—a most unspeakable advantage in business. On the other hand, let no complaisance, no gentleness of temper, no weak desire of pleasing on your part, no wheedling, coaxing, nor flattery, on other people's, make you recede, one jot, from any point which reason and prudence have bid you to pursue; but return to the charge, per-

* Gentleness of manner.

F

sist, persevere, and you will find most things attainable, that are possible. A yielding, timid meekness, is always insulted and abused, by the unjust and unfeeling; but when sustained by the *fortiter in re,** is always respected, commonly successful. In your friendships and connexions, as well as in your enmities, this rule is particularly useful; let your firmness and vigour preserve and invite attachments to you, but, at the same time, let your manner hinder the enemies of your friends and dependants from becoming yours: let your enemies be disarmed, by the gentleness of your manner; but let them feel, at the same time, the steadiness of your just resentment; for there is great difference between bearing malice, which is always ungenerous, and a resolute self-defence, which is always justifiable and prudent.

CHOICE OF COMPANY.

I HAVE advised you respecting your friends, and the knowledge of the world, let me now advise you respecting your COMPANY.

Endeavour, as much as you can, to keep good company, and the company of your superiors; for you will be held in estimation according to the company you keep. By superiors, I do not mean so much with regard to birth, as merit, and the light in which they are considered by the world.

To keep good company, especially at your first setting out, is the way to receive good

* Resolution.

impressions. If you ask me, what I mean by good company, I will confess to you, that it is pretty difficult to define; but I will endeavour to make you understand it.

Good company is not what certain sets of company are pleased either to call or think themselves; but it is that company which all the people of the place call, and acknowledge to be good company; notwithstanding some objections which they may form to some of the individuals who compose it. It consists chiefly (but by no means without exception) of people of considerable birth, rank, and character: for people of neither birth nor rank, are frequently, and very justly, admitted into it, if distinguished by any peculiar merit, or eminence in any liberal art or science. Nay, so motley a thing is good company, that many people, without birth, rank, or merit, intrude into it, by their own forwardness; and others slide into it by the protection of some considerable person; and some, even of indifferent characters and morals, make part of it. But, in the main, the good part preponderates, and people of infamous and blasted characters are never admitted. In this fashionable good company, the best manners, and the best language of the place, are most unquestionably to be learned; for they establish and give the tone to both, which are therefore called the language and manners of good company; there being no legal tribunal to ascertain either.

A company consisting wholly of people of the first quality, cannot, for that reason, be called good company, in the common acceptation of the phrase; unless they are, besides, the fashionable and accredited company of the place; for people of the very first quality, can be as silly, as ill bred, and as worthless, as people of the meanest degree. On the other hand, a company consisting entirely of people of very low condition, whatever their merit or parts may be, can never be called good company; and consequently should not be much frequented, though by no means despised.

But, in forming your estimate of company, do not let yourself be overpowered by fashion, nor by particular sets of people, with whom you may be connected: but try all the different coins, before you receive any in payment. Let your own good sense and reason, judge of the value of each; and be persuaded, that nothing can be beautiful, unless true. Whatever brilliancy is not the result of the solidity and justness of a thought, is but a false glare.

All this ought not to hinder you from conforming externally to the modes and tones of the different companies in which you may chance to be.

You may possibly ask me, whether a man has it always in his power to get into the best company? and how?—I say, Yes, he has, by deserving it; provided he is in circumstances which enable him to appear upon the footing of a gentleman. Merit and good breeding will make their way every where. Knowledge will introduce him, and good breeding will endear him to the best companies; for, as I have often told you, politeness and good breeding are absolutely necessary, to adorn any, or all other good qualities or talents. Without them, no knowledge, no perfection whatsoever, is seen in its best light. The scholar, without good breeding, is a pedant; the philosopher, a cynic; the soldier, a brute; and every man disagreeable.

A wit is a very unpopular denomination, as it carries terror along with it; and people in general are as much afraid of a live wit, in company, as a woman is of a gun; which she thinks may go off of itself, and do her a mischief. Their acquaintance is, however, worth seeking, and their company worth frequenting; but not exclusively of others, nor to such a degree as to be considered only as one of that particular set.

Frequent these people, and be glad, but not proud, of frequenting them; never boast of it, as a proof of your own merit; nor insult, in a manner, other companies, by telling them, affectedly, what you, Montesquieu and Fontenelle, were talking of the other day; as I have known many people do here, with regard to Pope and Swift, who had never been twice in company with either: nor carry into other companies the tone of those meetings of *beau esprits*.*

In selecting your company remember the Spanish saying, " Tell me with whom you live, and I will tell you who you are." Make it your business, wherever you are, to get into that company, which every body of the place allows to be the best company, next to their own: which is the best definition that I can give you of good company. But here, too, one caution is very necessary; for want of which, many young men have been ruined, even in good company. Good company (as I have before observed) is composed of a great variety of fashionable people, whose characters

* Gay spirits.

and morals are very different, though their manners are pretty much the same. When a young man, new in the world, first gets into that company, he very rightly determines to conform to, and imitate it. But then he too often, and fatally, mistakes the object of his imitation. He has often heard that absurd term of genteel and fashionable vices. He there sees some people who shine, and who in general are admired and esteemed; and observes, that these people are lascivious, drunkards, or gamesters: upon which, he adopts their vices; mistaking their defects for their perfections, and thinking that they owe their fashion and their lustre to these genteel vices. Whereas, it is exactly the reverse; for these people have acquired their reputation by their parts, their learning, their good breeding, and other real accomplishments; and are only blemished and lowered, in the opinion of all reasonable people, and of their own, in time, by these genteel and fashionable vices. A debauchee, suffering all the odious effect of his vices, is a very genteel person indeed, and well worthy of imitation! A drunkard, vomiting up, at night, the wine of the day, and stupified by the head-ache all the next, is doubtless, a fine model to copy from; and a gamester tearing his hair, and blaspheming, for having lost more than he had in the world, is surely a most amiable character!

Leave such persons to their ignorance, and to their dirty, disgraceful vices. They will severely feel their effects, when it will be too late. Without the comfortable refuge of opulence and titles, and with all the sickness and pains of a ruined stomach, and a rotten carcase, if they happen to arrive at old age, it is

an uneasy and ignominious one. The ridicule
which such fellows endeavour to throw upon
those who are not like them, is, in the opinion
of all men of sense, the most authentic
panegyric.

What I have now said, together with your
own good sense, is, I hope, sufficient to arm
you against the seduction, the invitations, or
the profligate exhortations, (for I cannot call
them temptations) of those unfortunate young
people. On the other hand, when they would
engage you in their schemes, content yourself with a decent but steady refusal. Avoid
controversy, upon such plain points. You are
too young, to convert them; and, I trust, too
wise to be converted by them. Shun them,
not only in reality, but even in appearance, if
you would be well received in good company;
for people will always be shy of receiving a
man, who comes from a place where the
plague rages, let him look ever so healthy.
There are some expressions, both in French
and English, and some characters, both in
those two and in other countries, which have,
I dare say, misled many young men to their
ruin—*Une honnête débauché, une jolie débauché;*
an agreeable rake, a man of pleasure. These
are phrases, invented, by the wicked and profligate, at once to conceal or excuse their own
vices, and to debauch others.

Be careful, therefore, in your choice of company; and nothing, I must observe, sinks a
young man into low company, both of women
and men, so surely as timidity, and diffidence
of himself. If he thinks that he shall not, he
may depend upon it he will not, please. But,
with proper endeavours to please, and a de-

gree of persuasion that he shall, it is almost certain that he will. How many people does one meet with, every where, who, with very moderate parts, and very little knowledge, push themselves pretty far, singly, by being sanguine, enterprising, and persevering? They will take no denial; difficulties do not discourage them; repulsed twice or thrice, they rally, they charge again, and, nine times in ten, prevail at last.

But the company which, of all others, you should carefully avoid, is that, which, in every sense of the word, may be called *low:* low in birth, low in rank, low in parts, and low in manners; that company, who, insignificant and contemptible in themselves, think it an honour to be seen with *you*, and who will flatter your follies, nay, your very vices, to keep you with them.

Though *you* may think such a caution unnecessary, I do not; for many a young gentleman of sense and rank, has been led, by his vanity, to keep such company, until he has been degraded, vilified, and undone.

The vanity I mean, is that of being the first of the company. This pride, though too common, is idle, to the last degree. Nothing in the world lets a man down so much. For the sake of dictating, being applauded and admired by this low company, he is disgraced, and disqualified for better. Depend upon it, in the estimation of mankind, you will sink or rise to the level of the company you keep.

Low company, and low pleasures, are always much more costly, than liberal and elegant ones. The disgraceful riots of a tavern, are much more expensive, as well as dishonourable, than the excesses in good company.

I must absolutely hear of no tavern scrapes and squabbles.

Be it, then, your ambition to get into the best company; and, when there, imitate their virtues, but not their vices. You have, no doubt, often heard of genteel and fashionable vices. These are, drinking, gaming, and frequenting houses of ill fame. It has happened, that some men, even with these vices, have been admired and esteemed. Understand this matter rightly. It is not their vices, for which they are admired, but for some accomplishments which they at the same time possess—their parts, their learning, or their good breeding. Be assured, were they free from their vices, they would be much more esteemed. In these mixed characters, the bad part is overlooked, for the sake of the good.

In mixed companies, whoever is admitted to make part of them, is, for the time, at least, supposed to be upon a footing of equality with the rest; and, consequently, as there is no one principal object of awe and respect, people are apt to take a greater latitude in their behaviour, and to be less upon their guard: and so they may, provided it be within certain bounds, which are upon no occasion to be transgressed. But, upon these occasions, though no one is entitled to distinguished marks of respect, every one claims, and very justly, every mark of civility and good breeding. Ease is allowed, but carelessness and negligence are strictly forbidden. If a man accosts you, and talks to you ever so dully or frivolously, it is worse than rudeness, it is brutality, to show him, by a manifest inattention to what he says, that you think him a fool or a blockhead, and not worth hearing. It is much more so, with regard to women; who, of whatever rank, are entitled, in consideration of their sex, not only to an attentive, but an officious good breeding, from men. Their little wants, likings, dislikes, preferences, antipathies, fancies, whims, and even impertinences, must be officiously attended to, flattered, and, if possible guessed at and anticipated, by a well bred man. You must never usurp, to yourself, those conveniences and *agrémens*,* which are of common right; such as the best places, the best dishes, &c.; but, on the contrary, always decline them, yourself, and offer them to others; who, in their turn, will offer them to you: so that, upon the whole, you will enjoy your share of the common right. It would be endless to enumerate all the particular instances in which a well bred man shows his good breeding, in good company; and it would be injurious to you, to suppose, that your own good sense will not point them out; and then, your own good nature will recommend, and your self-interest enforce the practice.

Should you be unfortunate enough to have any vices of your own, add not to their number, by adopting the vices of others. Vices of adoption are, of all others, the most unpardonable, for they have not inadvertency to plead. If people had no vices but their own, few would have so many as they have.

As I make no difficulty of confessing my past errors, where I think the confession may be of use to you, I will own, that, when I first went to the university, I drank and smoked,

* Preferences.

notwithstanding the aversion I had to wine and tobacco, only because I thought it genteel, and that it made me look like a man. When I went abroad, I first went to the Hague, where gaming was much in fashion; and where I observed that many people, of shining rank and character, gamed too. I was then young enough, and silly enough, to believe, that gaming was one of their accomplishments; and, as I aimed at perfection, I adopted gaming, as a necessary step to it. Thus, I acquired, by error, the habit of a vice, which, far from adorning my character, has, I am conscious, been a great blemish in it.

Imitate, then, with discernment and judgment, the real perfections of the good company, into which you may be introduced: copy their politeness, their carriage, their address, and the easy and well bred turn of their conversation; but remember, that, let them shine ever so bright, their vices, are so many spots, which you would no more imitate, than you would make an artificial wart upon your face, because some very handsome man had the misfortune to have a natural wart upon his; but, on the contrary, think how much handsomer he would have been, without it.

Every man becomes, to a certain degree, what the people are with whom he generally converses. He catches their air, their manners, and even their way of thinking. If he observes with attention, he will catch them soon; but if he does not, he will, in some time, insensibly contract them. I know nothing in the world but poetry, that is not to be acquired by application and care.

PLEASURE.

A WORD or two, on a subject to which all have a natural propensity, I mean PLEASURE.

When pleasure is made the chief pursuit of life, it will root out reason and reflection, and substitute in their room, impatience of thought and business. It moreover disappoints itself; and the constant application to it, palls our appetite for enjoyment.

Believe me, that the intermediate seasons of what is commonly called a man of pleasure, are more heavy and tormenting, than you would impose upon the vilest criminal. Take him when he is awakened from some debauch; and there is no man living, whose existence is a more insupportable burden to him. He is not to be easy, any longer than reflection is detained outside his curtains. Mortgages, diseases, and settlements, are his legacies. All the poor rogues that make such lamentable exits at Tyburn, were, once in their days, men of pleasure.

Were I certain that you were addicted to such a kind of pleasure, I could be still more grave, and should forewarn you of certain dishonour. I could tell you, that no man has ever been the slave of pleasure, that was not equally the slave of mean and overwhelming reflections.

And yet remember, pleasure is the rock upon which most young people split. They launch out, with crowded sails, in quest of it, but without a compass to direct their course, or reason sufficient to steer the vessel; for want of which, pain and shame, instead of pleasure, are the returns of their voyage. Do not think that I mean to snarl at pleasure, like a

stoic; no, I mean to point it out, and recommend it to you, like an epicurean: I wish you
a great deal; and my only view is to hinder
you from mistaking it.

The character at which most young men at
first aim is, that of a man of pleasure. But
they generally take it upon trust; and instead
of consulting their own taste and inclinations,
they blindly adopt whatever those with whom
they chiefly converse, are pleased to call by
the name of pleasure; and a man of pleasure,
in the vulgar acceptation of that phrase, means
only a beastly drunkard, a profligate swearer
and curser, and a wretched visiter of the bro-
thel. As it may be of use to you, I am not unwilling, though at the same time ashamed, to
own, that the vices of my youth proceeded
much more from my silly resolution of being
what I heard called a man of pleasure, than
from my own inclinations. I always naturally
hated drinking; and yet I have often drunk,
with disgust at the time, attended by great
sickness the next day, only because I then
considered drinking as a necessary qualification for a fine gentleman, and a man of pleasure.

I can say the same, as to gaming. I did
not want money, and consequently had no occasion to play for it: but I thought play another necessary ingredient in the composition
of a man of pleasure, and accordingly I plunged
into it, without desire, at first; sacrificed a
thousand real pleasures to it, and made myself solidly uneasy by it, for thirty of the best
years of my life.

I was even absurd enough, for a little while,
to swear, by way of adorning and completing
the shining character, which I affected; but

this folly I soon laid aside, upon finding both its indecency and guilt.

Thus seduced by fashion, and blindly adopting nominal pleasures, I lost real ones; and my fortune impaired, and my constitution shattered, are, I must confess, the just punishment of my errors.

Take warning, then, by them. Choose your pleasures for yourself, and let them not be imposed upon you by others. Weigh the present enjoyment of your pleasures, against their necessary consequences, and then let your own common sense determine your choice.

Those only who join serious occupations with pleasures, feel either, as they should do. An uninterrupted life of pleasure, is as insipid as contemptible. Some hours given every day to serious business, must whet both the mind and the senses, to enjoy those of pleasure. A surfeited glutton, an emaciated sot, and an enervated debauchee, never enjoy the pleasures to which they devote themselves. They are only so many human sacrifices to false gods. In short, pleasure must not, nay, cannot, be the business of a man of sense and character; but it may be, and is, his relief, his reward. It is particularly so, with regard to the women; who have the utmost contempt for those men, that, having no character nor consideration with their own sex, frivolously pass their whole time in *ruelles*, and at *toilettes*. They look upon them as their lumber, and remove them whenever they can get better furniture. Women choose their favourites more by the ear, than by any other of their senses, or even their understandings. The man whom they hear the most commended, by the men, will always be the best received by them.

LAUGHTER.

TRIFLING as the subject of LAUGHTER may appear, it is not beneath the attention of the man of breeding. Even philosophers have bestowed upon it a grave attention; and have held it be " a sudden glory, arising from a conception of our own superiority." But, whatever philosophers may be pleased to affirm respecting it, and however it may be regarded as one of the characteristics of man, when indulged in freely, it sinks the gentleman, into a very ordinary man.

Frequent and loud laughter, is the characteristic of folly and ill manners; it is the manner in which the mob express their silly joy, at silly things; and they call it being merry. In my mind, there is nothing so illiberal, and so ill bred, as audible laughter. True wit, or sense, never yet made any body laugh; they are above it: they please the mind, and give a cheerfulness to the countenance. But it is low buffoonery, or silly accidents, that always excite laughter; and that is what people of sense and breeding should show themselves above.

I do not recommend upon all occasions a solemn countenance. A man may smile, but if he would be thought a gentleman, and a man of sense, he should by no means laugh. True wit never made a man of fashion laugh; he is above it. It may create a smile, but a loud laughter shows that a man has not the command of himself; every one who would wish to appear sensible, must abhor it.

A man's going to sit down, on a supposition

that he has a chair behind him, and falling for want of one, occasions a general laugh, when the best pieces of wit could not do it; a sufficient proof how low and unbecoming laughter is.

Besides, could the immoderate laugher hear his own noise, or see the faces he makes, he would despise himself, for his folly. Laughter being generally supposed to be the effect of gaiety, its absurdity is not properly attended to; but a little reflection will easily restrain it, and when you are told it is a mark of low breeding, I persuade myself you will endeavour to avoid it.

Some people have a silly trick of laughing whenever they speak; so that they are always on the grin, and their faces ever distorted. This and a thousand other tricks, such as scratching their heads, twirling their hats, fumbling with their buttons, playing with their fingers, &c. &c. are acquired from a false modesty, at their first outset in life. Being shamefaced in company, they try a variety of ways to keep themselves in countenance; thus, they fall into those awkward habits which I have mentioned, which grow upon them, and in time become habitual.

Nothing is more repugnant, likewise, to good breeding, than horse-play of any sort, romping, throwing things at one another's heads, and so on. They may pass well enough with the mob, but they lessen and degrade the gentleman.

But, if you are to guard against immoderate laughter, much more are you to resist every attempt, in others, to make you the *butt* of the company. This is a character which may become one who sets up for a professed wit, or the buffoon of the company; or may sit easy enough upon a stupid fellow who has no objections to be laughed at; but nothing can be more grating, to the feelings of a man of honour. Take care to make people feel your superiority; at least behave in such a manner as to secure respect, and you shall never be selected as a butt.

DIGNITY OF MANNERS.

THERE is a certain DIGNITY OF MANNERS, without which the very best characters will not be valued.

Romping, loud and frequent laughing, punning, joking, mimicry, waggery, and too great and indiscriminate familiarity, will render any one contemptible, in spite of all his knowledge or his merit. These may constitute a merry fellow, but a merry fellow was never respectable. Indiscriminate familiarity, will either offend your superiors, or make you pass for their dependent or toad-eater, and it will put your inferiors on a degree of equality with you, that may be troublesome.

A joke, if it carries a sting along with it, is no longer a joke, but an affront; and, even if it has no sting, unless its witticism be delicate and facetious, instead of giving pleasure, it will disgust; or if the company *should* laugh, they will probably laugh at the jester rather than the jest.

Punning is a mere playing upon words, and far from being a mark of sense: thus, were we

to say such a dress is *commodious*, one of these
wags, would answer *odious;* or, that, whatever
it has been, it is now be *comm-odious.* Others
will give us an answer different from what we
should expect, without either wit, or the least
beauty of thought; as, *Where's my lord? In
his clothes, unless he is in bed. How does this
wine taste? A little moist, I think. How is
this to be eaten? With your mouth;* and so on:
all which (you will readily apprehend) is low
and vulgar. If your witticisms are not instantly approved by the laugh of the company,
for heaven's sake dont attempt to be witty for
the future; for you may take it for granted,
the defect is in yourself, and not in your
hearers.

As to a mimic or a wag, he is little else than
a buffoon, who will distort his mouth and his
eyes, to make people laugh. Be assured that
no one person ever demeaned himself to please
the rest, unless he wished to be thought the
Merry Andrew of the company: and whether
this character is respectable, I will leave you
to judge.

If a man's company be coveted on any other
account than his knowledge, his good sense,
or his manners, he is seldom respected by
those who invite him, but made use of only to
entertain. " Let's have such a one, for he
sings a good song, or he is always joking or
laughing;" or, " Let's send for such a one, for
he is a good bottle companion;" these are degrading distinctions, that preclude all respect
and esteem. Whoever is *had* (as the phrase
is) for the sake of any qualification singly, is
merely that thing he *is had* for, is never considered in any other light, and, of course,

never properly respected, let his intrinsic merits be what they will.

Not much more dignified, is the character of your young countrymen of quality, who distinguish themselves by the conduct of footmen and grooms.. But, with the manners of footmen and grooms, they assume their dress too. You must have observed them in the streets here, in dirty blue frocks, with oaken sticks in their hands, and their hair greasy and unpowdered, tucked up under their hats of an enormous size. Thus finished and adorned, by their travels, they become the disturbers of playhouses; they break the windows, and commonly the landlords, of the taverns where they drink; and are at once the support, the terror, and the victims, of the houses of ill fame, which they frequent. These poor mistaken people think they shine, and so they do indeed; but it is as putrefaction shines—in the dark.

Equally mistaken, are those poor young men who think to distinguish themselves by affecting the character of a rake. They too frequently and always fatally mistake that character for that of a man of pleasure; and always attach a false dignity to it. What a mistake! A rake is a composition of all the lowest, most ignoble, degrading and shameful vices. They all conspire to disgrace his character, to ruin his fortune, and most effectually destroy his constitution. A dissolute, flagitious footman, or porter, makes full as good a rake as a man of the first quality. By-the-bye, let me tell you, that, in the wildest part of my youth, I never was a rake, but on the contrary, always detested and despised the character.

This dignity of manners, which I recommend so much to you, is not only as different from pride, as true courage is from blustering, or true wit from joking; but is absolutely inconsistent with it; for nothing vilifies and degrades more than pride. The pretensions of the proud man, are oftener treated with sneer and contempt, than with indignation; as we offer ridiculously too little to a tradesman, who asks ridiculously too much for his goods; but we do not haggle with one, who asks only a just and reasonable price.

Abject flattery and indiscriminate assentation degrade, as much as indiscriminate contradiction and noisy debate, disgust. But a modest assertion of one's own opinion, and a complaisant acquiescence in other people's, preserve dignity.

Vulgar, low expressions, awkward motions and address, vilify, as they imply, either a very low turn of mind, or low education, and low company.

Frivolous curiosity about trifles, and a laborious attention to little objects, which neither require nor deserve a moment's thought, lower a man; who from thence is thought (and not unjustly) incapable of greater matters. Cardinal de Retz, very sagaciously marked out Cardinal Chigi for a little mind, from the moment he told him he had written three years with the same pen, and that it was an excellent good one still.

A certain degree of exterior seriousness in looks and motions, gives dignity, without excluding wit and decent cheerfulness, which are always serious themselves. A constant smirk upon the face, and a whiffling activity of the body, are strong indications of futility. Whoever is in a hurry, shows that the thing he is about is too big for him.

To form dignity of character, advantageously, you have three objects particularly to attend to; your character as a man of morality, of truth, and of honour; your knowledge in the objects of your destination, as a man of business; and your engaging and insinuating address, air, and manners—the sure and only steps to favour. Merit, at courts, without favour, will do little or nothing; favour, without merit, will do a good deal; but favour and merit together, will do every thing.

As to the first, see that you are exceedingly careful and jealous of the dignity of your character: that is the sure and solid foundation upon which you must both stand and rise.

There is nothing so delicate, as your moral character; and nothing that it is your interest so much to preserve pure. Should you be suspected of injustice, malignity, perfidy, lying, &c. all the parts and knowledge in the world, will never procure you esteem, friendship, or respect. A strange concurrence of circumstances has sometimes raised very bad men to high stations; but they have been raised like criminals to a pillory, where their persons and their crimes, by being more conspicuous, are only the more known, the more detested, and the more pelted and insulted. If, in any case, whatsoever, dissimulation is pardonable, it is in the case of morality; though even there, I would not advise you to a Pharasaical pomp of virtue. But I will recommend to you a most scrupulous tenderness for your moral character, and the utmost care not to say or do the least thing, that may, ever so slightly, taint it. Show yourself, upon all occasions, the advocate, the friend, but not the bully, of virtue.

Labour to possess strength of mind. The sure characteristic of a sound and strong mind, is, to find, in every thing, those certain bounds, *quos ultra citraque nequit consistere rectum.** These boundaries are marked out by a very fine line, which only good sense and attention can discover. It is much too fine, for vulgar eyes. In manners, this line is good breeding; beyond it, is troublesome ceremony; short of it, is unbecoming negligence and inattention. In morals, it divides ostentatious puritanism, from criminal relaxation; in religion, superstition from impiety; and, in short, every virtue from its kindred vice or weakness. I think you have sense enough to discover the line: keep it always in your eye, and learn to walk upon it.

Your address and manner are no less requisite, to form the basis of dignity of character. A perfect self-command, a knowledge of the customary rules of good breeding, and assurance with ease, are necessary ingredients in the composition of dignity. A certain firmness must accompany all our actions. A mean, timid, and passive complaisance, degrades a man, more than he is aware of; but still his firmness and resolution should not extend to brutality, but be accompanied with a peculiar and engaging mildness.

I see no impudence, but, on the contrary, in-

---

* On either side of which, there is an extreme.

finite utility and advantage, in presenting
one's-self with the same coolness and unconcern, in any, and every company. Till one
can do that, I am very sure that one can never
present one's-self well. Whatever is done
under concern and embarrassment, must be
ill done; and, till a man is absolutely easy and
unconcerned, in every company, he will never
be thought to have kept good, nor to be wel-.
come in it. A steady assurance, with seeming
modesty, is possibly the most useful qualification that a man can have in every part of life.
A man would certainly make a very inconsi-
derable fortune and figure in the world, whose
modesty and timidity should often, as bashfulness always does, put him in the deplorable
and lamentable situation of the pious Æneas,
when *obstupuit, steteruntque comæ, et vox fau-
cibus hæsifit.** Fortune (as well as women)

   ——Born to be controll'd,
 Stoops to the forward and the bold.

Firmness and intrepidity, under the white
banner of real, but not awkward modesty, clear
the way for merit, that would otherwise be
discouraged by difficulties in its journey; whereas, barefaced impudence is the noisy and blustering harbinger of a worthless and senseless
usurper.

 People of a low, obscure education, cannot
stand the rays of greatness. They are frightened out of their wits, when kings and great
men speak to them; they are awkward,
ashamed, and do not know what nor how to

---

* He was amazed; his hair stood on end,
and his voice clung to his jaws.

answer; whereas, *les honnêtes gens** are not dazzled by superior rank: they know and pay all the respect that is due to it; but they do it without being disconcerted; and can converse just as easily with a king, as with any one of his subjects. That is the great advantage of being introduced young into good company; and being used early to converse with one's superiors. How many men have I seen here, who, after having had the full benefit of an English education, first at school, and then at the university, when they have been presented to the king, did not know whether they stood upon their heads or their heels? If the king spoke to them, they were annihilated; they trembled, endeavoured to put their hands into their pockets, and missed them, let their hats fall, and were ashamed to take them up; and, in short, put themselves in every attitude but the right, that is, the easy and natural one. The characteristic of a well bred man, is, to converse with his inferiors without insolence, and with his superiors with respect, and with ease. He talks to kings, without concern; he trifles with women of the first condition with familiarity, gaiety, but respect; and converses with his equals, whether he is acquainted with them or not, upon general common topics, that are not, however, quite frivolous, without the least concern of mind, or awkwardness of body; neither of which can appear to advantage but when it is perfectly easy.

Were you to converse with a king, you ought to be as easy and unembarrassed, as with your own valet de chambre: yet every

---

* People of fashion.

look, word, and action, should imply the utmost respect. What would be proper and well bred, with others, much your superiors, would be absurd and ill bred with one so very much so. You must wait till you are spoken to; you must receive, not give, the subject of conversation; and you must even take care that the given subject of such conversation, do not lead you into any impropriety. Almost the same precautions are necessary to be used with ministers, generals, &c. who expect to be treated with very nearly the same respect as their masters, and commonly deserve it better. There is, however, this difference, that one may begin the conversation with them, if on their side it should happen to drop, provided one does not carry it to any subject upon which it is improper either for them to speak or be spoken to. In these two cases, certain attitudes and actions would be extremely absurd, because too easy, and consequently disrespectful. As for instance, if you were to put your arms across in your bosom, twirl your snuff-box, trample with your feet, scratch your head, &c. it would be shockingly ill bred in that company, and, indeed, not extremely well bred, in any other. The great difficulty, in those cases, though a very surmountable one, by attention and custom, is to join perfect inward ease, with perfect outward respect.

A passionate temper lowers a man exceedingly, and is perfectly incompatible with the dignity of manners which I am here recommending. If you discover any hastiness in your temper, and find it apt to break out into rough and unguarded expressions, watch it narrowly, and endeavour to curb it; but let no complaisance, no weak desire of pleasing, no wheedling, urge you to do that which discretion forbids; but persist and persevere in all that is right. In your connexions and friendships, you will find this rule of use to you. Invite and preserve attachments, by your firmness: but labour to keep clear of enemies, by a mildness of behaviour. Disarm those enemies you may unfortunately have, (and few are without them) by a gentleness of manner; but make them feel the steadiness of your just resentment: for there is a wide difference between bearing malice, and a determined self-defence; the one is imperious, but the other is prudent and justifiable.

In directing your servants, or any person that you have a right to command, if you deliver your orders mildly, and in that engaging manner which every gentleman should study to do, you will be cheerfully, and consequently, well obeyed; but if tyrannically, you will be very unwillingly served, if served at all. A cool, steady determination should show that you will be obeyed, but a gentleness in the manner of enforcing that obedience, should make service a cheerful one. Thus, will you be beloved, without being despised, and feared without being hated.

I hope I need not mention vices. A man who has patiently been kicked out of company, may have as good a pretence to courage, as one rendered infamous by his vices, may to dignity of any kind. A tradesman who would succeed in his way, must begin by establishing a character of integrity and good manners: without the former, nobody will go to his shop at all; without the latter, nobody will go there

twice. This rule does not exclude the fair
arts of trade. He may sell his goods at the
best price he can, within certain bounds. He
may avail himself of the humour, the whims,
and the fantastical tastes, of his customers;
but what he warrants to be good, must be
really so; what he seriously asserts, must be
true: or his first fraudulent profits will soon
end in bankruptcy. It is the same, in higher
life, and in the great business of the world. A
man who does not solidly establish, and really
deserve, a character of truth, probity, good
manners, and good morals, at his first setting
out in the world, may impose, and shine, like a
meteor, for a very short time; but will very
soon vanish, and be extinguished, with contempt. People may pardon, in young men,
the common irregularities of the senses; but
they do not forgive the least vice of the heart.
The heart never grows better, by age; I fear
rather worse; always harder. A young liar
will be an old one; and a young knave will
only be a greater knave, as he grows older.
But should a bad young heart, accompanied
with a good head (which, by the way, very
seldom is the case) really reform, in a more
advanced age, from a consciousness of its folly,
as well as of its guilt, such a conversion would
only be thought prudential and political, but
never sincere. The possession of all the moral virtues, *in actu primo*,* as the logicians call
it, is not sufficient; you must have them in
actu secundo† too. Nay, that is not sufficient,
neither; you must have the reputation of

---

* Of the first class.　　† Of the second.

them, also. Your character in the world must
be built upon that solid foundation, or it will
soon fall, and upon your own head. You cannot, therefore, be too careful, too nice, too scrupulous, in establishing this character, at first,
upon which your whole depends. Let no conversation, no example, no fashion, no *bon mot,**
no silly desire of seeming to be above what
most knaves, and many fools, call prejudices,
ever tempt you to avow, excuse, extenuate, or
laugh at, the least breach of morality; but
show, upon all occasions, and take all occasions to show, a detestation and abhorrence of
it. There, though young, you ought to be
strict; and there only, while young, it becomes
you to be strict and severe. But there, too,
spare the persons, while you lash the crimes.

Pray let no quibbles of lawyers, no refine-
ments of casuists, break into the plain notions
of right and wrong, which every man's right
reason, and plain common sense suggest to
him. To do as you would be done by, is the
plain, sure, and undisputed rule of morality
and justice. Adhere to that, and be convinced,
that whatever infringes it, in any degree, however speciously it may be turned, and however
puzzling it may be to answer it, is, notwithstanding, false in itself, unjust, and criminal.

It is even necessary, that you should have
religion. Depend upon it, that nine-tenths of
mankind, should you be given out as a pro-
fane man, or an atheist, will entertain an opinion of you, derogatory to dignity of character. Goodness is real greatness. Religion
will lay the most solid basis of true dignity,

---

* Witty saying.

and without it, neither titles nor opulence will support a character long.

When I speak of religion, I do not mean that you should talk or act like a missionary, or an enthusiast, nor that you should take up a controversial cudgel against every one that attacks the sect you are of. This would be both useless and unbecoming your age. But I mean that you should by no means seem to approve, encourage, or applaud, those libertine notions, which strike at religions equally, and which are the poor threadbare topics of half-wits, and self-created philosophers. Even those who are silly enough to laugh at their jokes, are still wise enough to distrust and detest their characters: for, putting moral virtues at the highest, and religion at the lowest, religion must still be allowed to be, at least, a great collateral security to virtue; and every prudent man will sooner trust to two securities, than to one. Whenever, therefore, you happen to be in company with those pretended *esprits forts*,* or with thoughtless libertines, who laugh at all religion, to show their wit, or disclaim it, to complete their riot, let no word or look of yours intimate the least approbation; on the contrary, let a silent gravity express your dislike; but enter not into the subject, and decline such unprofitable and indecent controversies. Depend upon this truth —that every man is the worse looked upon, and the less trusted, for being thought to have no religion; in spite of all the pompous and specious epithets he may assume, of *esprit fort*, free-thinker, or moral philosopher; and a wise atheist (if such a thing there is) would, for his

* Daring spirits.

own interest, and character in this world, pretend to some religion.

But if you should, unfortunately, have no intrinsic merit of your own, keep up, if possible, the appearance of it; and the world will possibly give you credit for the rest. A versatility of manners is as necessary in social life, as a versatility of parts, in political. This is no way blameable, if not used with an ill design. We must, like the chameleon, often put on the hue of the persons whose good opinion we esteem : and it surely can never be blameable, to endeavour to gain the good will or affection of any one, if, when obtained, we do not mean to abuse it.

IMPROVEMENT.

I HAVE so often recommended to you attention and application to whatever you learn, that I do not mention them now as duties; but I point them out, as conducive, nay, absolutely necessary to your pleasures; for can there be a greater pleasure, than to be universally allowed to excel those of one's own age and manner of life? Consequently, can there be any thing more mortifying, than to be excelled by them? I do not confine the application which I recommend, singly to the view and emulation of excelling others (though this is a very sensible pleasure, and a very warrantable pride) but I mean likewise to excel in the thing itself; for, in my mind, one may as well not know a thing at all, as know it but imperfectly. To know a little of any thing, gives neither satisfaction nor credit; but often brings disgrace or ridicule.

In all systems, whatsoever, whether of religion, government, morals, &c. perfection is the object always proposed, though possibly unattainable; hitherto, at least, certainly unattained. However, those who aim carefully at the mark itself, will unquestionably come nearer to it, than those who, from despair, negligence, or indolence, leave to chance the work of skill. This maxim holds equally true, in common life. Those who aim at perfection, will come nearer to it, than those desponding, or indolent spirits, who foolishly say to themselves, " Nobody is perfect; perfection is unattainable; to attempt it, is chimerical; I shall do as well as others; why, then, should I give myself trouble to be what I never can, and what, according to the common course of things, I need not be—*perfect?"*

I am very sure that I need not point out to you the weakness and the folly of this reasoning, if it deserves the name of reasoning. It would discourage, and put a stop to the exertion of any one of our faculties. On the contrary, a man of sense and spirit says to himself, though the point of perfection may (considering the imperfection of our nature) be unattainable, " My care, my endeavours, my attention, shall not be wanting to get as near to it as I can."

It is my wish to aid you in a resolution so laudable. I do not mean that you are to aim at perfection, in every study in which you may embark. Many of these are intended only as the scaffolding, to the erection and completion of a more useful building. But mental labour is necessary, even in the less requisite parts.

Use and assert your own reason. Reflect, examine, and analyze, every thing, in order to form a sound and mature judgment; let no *ᴧτος ερα** impose upon your understanding, mislead your actions, or dictate your conversation. Be early, what, if you are not, you will, when too late, wish you had been. Consult your reason, betimes: I do not say that it will always prove an unerring guide: for human reason is not infallible: but it will prove the least erring guide that you can follow, except holy writ. Books and conversation may assist it; but adopt neither, blindly and implicitly: try both by that rule, which God has given to direct us—reason. Of all the troubles, do not decline, as many people do, that of thinking. The herd of mankind can hardly be said to think; their notions are almost all adopted.

Ask questions, and many questions, and leave nothing till you are thoroughly informed of it. Such pertinent questions are far from being ill bred, or troublesome, to those of whom you ask them; on the contrary, they are a tacit compliment to their knowledge; and people have a better opinion of a young man, when they see him desirous to be informed.

I wish you would use yourself to translate every day, only three or four lines, from any book, in any language, into the most correct and elegant English that you can think of. You cannot imagine how it will insensibly form your style, and give you an habitual elegancy: it would not take you up a quarter of an hour in a day.

---

* *Ipse dixit*—dogmatical assertion.

Acquire a general notion of astronomy and geometry; of both which, you may know as much as I desire you should, in six months time. I only wish that you shall have a clear notion of the present planetary system, and the history of all the former systems. Fontenelle's *Pluralité des Mondes** will teach you nearly all you need know, upon that subject. As for geometry, the first seven books of Euclid will be a sufficient portion of it for you. It is right, to have a general notion of those abstruse sciences, so as not to appear quite ignorant of them, when they happen, as sometimes they do, to be the topics of conversation; but a deep knowledge of them requires too much time, and engrosses the mind too much. Take the shortest general history you can find, of every country, and mark down in that history the most important periods, such as conquests, changes of kings, and alterations of the form of government; and then have recourse to more extensive histories, or particular treatises, relative to these great points. Consider them well, trace up their causes, and follow their consequences.

A taste for sculpture and painting, is, in my mind, as becoming, as a taste for fiddling and piping is unbecoming, a man of fashion. The former is connected with history and poetry; the latter, with nothing that I know of, but bad company.

That you may do all this the better, let me recommend to you attention and method. Without attention, all your labour will be spent to no purpose. It signifies nothing to read a

---

* Plurality of worlds.

g 2

thing once, if one does not mind and remember it. It is a sure sign of a little mind, to be doing one thing, and at the same time to be either thinking of another, or not thinking at all. One should always think of what one is about. When one is learning, one should not think of play; and when one is at play, one should not think of one's learning.

Be sure that you not only read, but that you think and reflect upon what you read. Many great readers load their memories, without exercising their judgments; and make lumber-rooms of their heads, instead of furnishing them usefully: facts are heaped upon facts, without order or distinction, and may justly be said to compose that

> ———— Rudis indigest aque moles
> Quam dixere chaos.*

Take nothing for granted, upon the bare authority of the author; but weigh and consider, in your own mind, the probability of the facts, and the justness of the reflections. Consult different authors upon the same facts, and form your opinion upon the greater or lesser degree of probability arising from the whole; which, in my mind, is the utmost stretch of historical faith; certainty (I fear) not being to be found. When an historian pretends to give you the causes and motives of events, compare those causes and motives with the characters and interests of the parties concerned, and judge for yourself, whether they correspond or not. Consider whether you cannot assign others,

---

* A rude and unformed mass, which they call chaos.

more probable; and, in that examination, do not despise some very mean and trifling causes of the actions of great men: for so various and inconsistent is human nature, so strong and so changeable are our passions, so fluctuating are our wills, and so much are our minds influenced by the accidents of our bodies, that every man is more the man of the day, than a regular and consequential character. The best have something bad, and something little; the worst have something good, and sometimes something great.

There are a great many people, who think themselves employed all day, and who, if they were to cast up their accounts at night, would find that they had done just nothing. They have read two or three hours, mechanically, without either attending to what they read, and, consequently, without retaining it, or reasoning upon it. Thence, they saunter into company, without taking any part in it, and without observing the characters of the persons, or the subjects of the conversation; but are either thinking of some trifle, foreign to the present purpose, or, often, not thinking at all; which silly and idle suspension of thought they would dignify with the name of absence and distraction.

Be as attentive to your pleasures, as to your studies. In the latter, observe and reflect upon all you read: in the former, be watchful and attentive to all that you see and hear; and never have it to say, as a thousand fools do, of things that were said and done before their faces, "That, truly, they did not mind them, because they were thinking of something else." Why were they thinking of something

else? and, if they were, why did they come
there? The truth is, that the fools were thinking of nothing. Remember to do what you
are about, well, be that what it will; it is
either worth doing well, or not at all.

But, whether it regards study or business, I
heartily wish you would immediately begin to
be a man of method; nothing contributing
more to facilitate and despatch business, than
method and order. Have order and method in
your accounts, in your reading, in the allot-
ment of your time; in short, in every thing.
You cannot conceive how much time you will
save by it, nor how much better every thing
you do will be done.

Prevail with yourself to observe good method and order only for one fortnight; and I
will venture to assure you, that you will never
neglect them afterward, you will find such
convenience and advantage arising from them.
Method is the great advantage that lawyers have
over other people, in speaking in Parliament:
for, as they must necessarily observe it in their
pleadings, in the courts of justice, it becomes
habitual to them, every where else.

Despatch is the soul of business, and nothing
contributes more to despatch, than method.
Lay down a method for every thing, and adhere to it, inviolably, as far as unexpected incidents may allow. Fix one certain hour and
day in the week for your accounts, and keep
them together, in their proper order; by which
means, they will require very little time, and
you can never be much cheated. Whatever
letters and papers you keep, label and tie
them in their respective classes, so that you
may instantly have recourse to any one. Lay

down a method also for your reading, for which
you allot a certain share of your mornings;
let it be in a consistent and consecutive course,
and not in that desultory and immethodical
manner, in which many people read scraps of
different authors, upon different subjects.
Keep a short common-place book of what you
read, to help your memory only, and not for
pedantic quotations. Never read history without having maps, and a chronological book, or
tables, lying by you, and constantly recurred
to; without which, history is only a confused
heap of facts. One method more I recommend to you, by which I have found great benefit, even in the most dissipated part of my
life; that is, to rise early, and at the same
hour every morning, how late soever you may
have sat up the night before. This secures
you an hour or two, at least, of reading or reflection, before the common interruptions of
the morning begin; and it will save your constitution, by forcing you to go to bed early, at
least one night in three.

EMPLOYMENT OF TIME.

Employment of Time is a subject, that,
from its importance, deserves your best attention. Most young gentlemen have a great
deal of time before them; and one hour well
employed in the early part of life, is more valuable, and will be of greater use to you, than
perhaps four-and-twenty some years to come.
A minute is precious to you now; whole days
may possibly not be so forty years hence.

I most earnestly recommend to you the care of those minutes and quarters of hours, in the course of the day, which people think too short to deserve their attention; and yet, if summed up, at the end of the year, would amount to a very considerable portion of time. For example: you are to be at such a place at twelve, by appointment; you go out at eleven, to make two or three visits first; those persons are not at home: instead of sauntering away that intermediate time at a coffee-house, and possibly alone, return home, write a letter, before-hand, for the ensuing post, or take up a good book; I do not mean Descartes, Mallebranche, Locke, or Newton, by way of dipping; but some book of rational amusement, and detached pieces, as Horace, Boileau, Waller, La Bruyere, &c. This will be so much time saved, and by no means ill employed. Many people lose a great deal of time by reading: for they read frivolous and idle books; such as absurd romances and novels; where characters, that never existed, are insipidly displayed, and sentiments, that were never felt, pompously described: the oriental ravings and extravagances of the Arabian Nights, and Mogul Tales: or, the new flimsy *brochures** that now swarm in France, of fairy tales, *Réflections sur le Cœur et l'Esprit, Métaphysique de l'Amour, Analyse des beaux Sentiments;*† and such sort of idle and frivolous stuff, that nourishes and improves the mind

---

* Pamphlets.

† Reflections upon the Heart and the Soul; The Metaphysics of Love; Analysis of Fine Sentiments.

just as much as whipped cream would the body. Throw away none of your time upon those trivial, futile, corrupting books, published by idle, vicious, or necessitous authors, for the amusement of idle or ignorant readers: such sort of books swarm and buzz about one every day; flap them away, they have no sting. *Certum pete finem,** have some one object for those leisure moments, and pursue that object, invariably, till you have attained it; and then take some other. A man of sense knows how to make the most of time, and puts out his whole sum, either to interest or to pleasure. He is never idle; but constantly employed either in amusements or in study.

Whatever time you can steal from company, and from the study of the world, (I say company, for a knowledge of life is best learned in various companies) employ it in serious reading. Take up some valuable book, and continue the reading of that book till you have got through it; never burden your mind with more than one thing at a time. In reading this book, do not run over it superficially, but read every passage twice over, at least do not pass on to a second, until you thoroughly understand the first, nor quit the book until you are master of the subject. By these means, (to use a city metaphor) you will make fifty *per cent.* of that time, of which others do not make above three or four, or probably nothing at all.

Many people lose a great deal of their time, by laziness. They loll and yawn in a great chair, tell themselves that they have not time

---

* Have a certain object in view.

to begin any thing then, and that it will do as well another time. This is a most unfortunate disposition, and the greatest obstruction to both knowledge and business. At your age. you have no right nor claim to laziness. I have, if I please, being *emeritus*.* You are but just listed in the world, and must be active, diligent, and indefatigable. If ever you propose commanding with dignity, you must serve up to it with diligence. Never put off till to-morrow, what you can do to-day.

Very few people are good economists of their fortunes, and still fewer of their time ; and yet, of the two, the latter is the most precious. Young people are apt to think they have so much time before them, that they may squander what they please of it; and yet have enough left; as very great fortunes have frequently seduced people to a ruinous profusion.

Many people think that they are in pleasures, provided they are neither in study nor in business. Nothing like it; they are doing nothing, and might just as well be asleep. They contract habitudes from laziness, and they frequent only those places where they are free from all restraints and attentions. Be upon your guard, against this idle profusion of time ; and let every place you go to, be either the scene of rational and lively pleasures, or the school of your improvements: let every company you go into, either gratify your senses, extend your knowledge, or refine your manners. Have some rational object of amusement in view, at some places; frequent others, where people of wit and taste assemble; get

* Finished—graduated.

into others, where people of superior rank and
dignity command respect and attention from
the rest of the company; but pray frequent no
neutral places, from mere idleness and indolence. Nothing forms a young man so much,
as being used to keep respectable and superior company, where constant regard and attention is necessary. It is true, this is at first
a disagreeable state of restraint; but it soon
grows habitual, and consequently easy; and
you are amply paid for it, by the improvement that you make, and the credit that it
gives you. Be curious, attentive, inquisitive,
as to every thing; listlessness and indolence
are always blameable; but, at your age, they
are unpardonable. Consider how precious,
and how important for all the rest of your life,
are your moments for these next three or four
years, and do not lose one of them. Do not
think I mean that you should study all day
long; I am far from advising or desiring it:
but I desire that you would be doing something or other, all day long; and not neglect
half hours and quarters of hours, which, at the
year's end, amount to a great sum. For instance, there are many short intervals in the
day, between studies and pleasures: instead
of sitting idle and yawning, in those intervals,
take up any book, though ever so trifling a
one, even down to a jest book; it is still better than doing nothing. I knew once a very
covetous sordid fellow, who used frequently to
say, " Take care of the pence; for the pounds
will take care of themselves." This was a
just and sensible reflection, in a miser. I recommend to you to take care of minutes; for
hours will take care of themselves. I am very

sure that many people lose two or three hours every day, by not taking care of the minutes. Never think any portion of time whatsoever too short, to be employed: something or other may always be done in it.

Any business you may have to transact, should be done the first opportunity, and finished, if possible, without interruption. Business must not be sauntered and trifled with; and you must not say to it, as Felix did to Paul, "at a more convenient season, I will speak to thee." The most convenient season for business, is the first; but study and business, in some measure, point out their own times to a man of sense. Business, of any kind, should never be done by halves, but every part of it should be well attended to; for he that does business ill, had better not do it at all: and, in any point that discretion bids you pursue, and that has a manifest utility to recommend it, let not difficulties deter you; rather let them animate your industry. If one method fails, try a second, and a third. Be active, persevere, and you will certainly conquer.

Husband your time, and make the best of it, every where. When you are in company, bring the conversation to some useful subject, but *à portée** of that company. Points of history, matters of literature, the customs of particular countries, the several orders of knighthood, as Teutonic, Maltese, &c. are surely better subjects of conversation, than the weather, dress, or fiddle-faddle stories, that carry no information along with them. The characters of kings and great men, are to be learned

---

* Within the capacity.

only in conversation; for they are never fairly written, during their lives. This, therefore, is an entertaining, instructive subject of conversation; and will likewise afford you an opportunity of observing how very differently characters are given, from the different passions and views of those who give them.

All those things, in the common course of life, depend entirely upon the manner; and, in that respect, the vulgar saying is true, " That one man may better steal a horse, than another look over the hedge." There are few things that may not be said, in some manner or other: either in a seeming confidence, or a genteel irony, or introduced with wit: and, one great part of the knowledge of the world, consists in knowing when, and where, to make use of these different manners. The graces of the person, of the countenance, and the way of speaking, contribute so much to this, that I am convinced, the very same thing, said by a genteel person, in an engaging way, and gracefully and distinctly spoken, would please—which would shock, if muttered out by an awkward figure, with a sullen, serious countenance. The poets always represent Venus as attended by the three Graces; to intimate, that even beauty will not do without them. I think they should have given Minerva three also; for without them, I am sure, learning is very unattractive. Invoke them, then, distinctly, to accompany all your words and actions.

I look back, with regret, upon that large sum of time, which, in my youth, I lavished away idly, without either improvement or pleasure.

Were I to begin the world again, with the

experience which I now have of it, I would lead a life of real, not of imaginary pleasure. I would enjoy the pleasures of the table, and of wine; but stop short of the pains inseparably annexed to an excess in either. I would not, at twenty years, be a preaching missionary of abstemiousness and sobriety; and I should let other people do as they would, without formally and sententiously rebuking them for it; but I would be most firmly resolved not to destroy my own faculties and constitution, in complaisance to those who have no regard to their own. I would play to give me pleasure, but not to give me pain; that is, I would play for trifles, in mixed companies, to amuse myself, and conform to custom; but I would take care not to venture for sums, which, if I won, I should not be the better for; but, if I lost, should be under a difficulty to pay; and, when paid, would oblige me to retrench, in several other articles: not to mention the quarrels that are commonly occasioned by deep play.

I would pass some of my time in reading, and the rest in the company of people of sense and learning, and chiefly those above me: and I would frequent the mixed companies of men and women of fashion; which, though often frivolous, yet unbend and refresh the mind, not uselessly, because they certainly polish and soften the manners.

Take warning betimes, and employ every moment; the longest life is too short for knowledge, consequently every moment is precious.

ECONOMY.

THERE is a discreet management of money, which I would not have you overlook. It is a habit which is alike remote from avarice and prodigality; and is absolutely requisite to enable one to pass through the world respectably.

There cannot be a more unhappy disposition, than that which hurries a man into debt. One would think it impossible that such a man should know, that his creditor has it in his power to say of him, after he has broken his word, the worst thing that can be said, *that he is unjust;* and can seize upon his person, without being guilty of an assault.

The want of economy blights many a fair character in the bud, and renders a man useless all the rest of his life. The consequences of prodigality, are excessively degrading. Can there be a more servile condition, than to be ashamed or afraid to see any man breathing? Yet the extravagant man is in that situation, with perhaps half the people he meets.

You will find many examples of this kind, among those who have high pretensions to honour. Their situation were to be pitied, had misfortune reduced them to that state. But this is not the case; it is caused by their extravagance. The father mortgages, and the son redeems it by marriage, and mortgages in his turn; and thus the infamous practice descends, by a kind of hereditary succession.

On the contrary, nothing has a more happy influence upon a man's fortune, than economy. It augments wealth, and you ought never to forget, that wealth is power.

The Duke de Sully observes very justly, in his Memoirs, that nothing contributed more to his rise, than that prudent economy, which he had observed from his youth; and by which he had always a sum of money before-hand, in case of emergencies.

It is very difficult, to fix the particular point of economy : the best error of the two is on the parsimonious side. That may be corrected; the other cannot.

The reputation of generosity is to be purchased pretty cheap. It does not depend so much upon a man's general expense, as upon his giving handsomely, where it is proper to give at all. A man, for instance, who should give a servant four shillings, would pass for covetous, while he who gave him a crown, would be reckoned generous: so that the difference of these two opposite characters, turns upon one shilling. A man's character, in that particular, depends a great deal upon the report of his own servants: a mere trifle above common wages makes their report favourable.

A fool squanders away, without credit or advantage to himself, more than a man of sense spends with both. The latter employs his money as he does his time, and never spends a shilling of the one, nor a minute of the other, but in something that is either useful or rationally pleasing to himself or others. The former buys whatever he does not want, and does not pay for what he does want. He cannot withstand the charms of a toy-shop; snuff-boxes, watches, heads of canes, &c. are his destruction. His servants and tradesmen conspire with his own indolence, to cheat him; and, in a very little time, he is astonished, in

.he midst of all the ridiculous superfluities, to ind himself in want of all the real comforts ınd necessaries of life. Without care and me.hod, the largest fortune will not, and with :hem, almost the smallest will supply, all neɔessary expenses. As far as you can possibly, ɔay ready money, for every thing you buy, and ıvoid bills. Pay that money, too, yourself, and not through the hands of any servant; who always either stipulates poundage, or requires a present for his good word, as they call it. Where you must have bills (as for meat and drink, clothes, &c.) pay them regularly every month, and with your own hand. Never, from a mistaken economy, buy a thing you do not want, because it is cheap; or, from a silly pride, because it is dear. Keep an account, in a book, of all that you receive, and of all that you pay; for no man, who knows what he receives, and what he pays, ever runs out.

SUNDRY LITTLE ACCOMPLISHMENTS.

I HAVE had reason to observe, before, that various little matters, apparently trifling in themselves, conspire to form the whole of pleasing, as in a well. finished portrait, a variety of colours combine to complete the piece. It not being necessary to dwell much upon them, I shall content myself with just mentioning them as they occur.

To do the honours of a table gracefully, is one of the outlines of a well bred man; and to carve well, is an article, little as it may seem,

that is useful twice every day, and the doing
of which ill, is not only troublesome to one's-
self, but renders us disagreeable and ridiculous
to others. We are always in pain for a man,
who instead of cutting up a fowl genteelly, is
hacking for half an hour across the bone,
greasing himself, and bespattering the company with the sauce. Use, with a little attention, is all that is requisite to acquit yourself
well, in this particular.

To be well received, you must also pay
some attention to your behaviour at table;
where it is exceedingly rude to scratch any
part of your body, to spit, or blow your nose,
if you can possibly avoid it, to eat greedily, to
lean your elbows on the table, to pick your
teeth before the dishes are removed, or to
leave the table before grace is said.

Drinking of healths is now growing out of
fashion, and is very impolite in good company.
Custom had once made it universal, but the
improved manners of the age, now render it
vulgar. What can be more rude or ridiculous,
than to interrupt persons at their meals, with
an unnecessary compliment? Abstain, then,
from this silly custom, where you find it out of
use; and use it only at those tables where it
continues general.

A polite manner of refusing to comply with
the solicitations of a company, is also very necessary to be learned; for, a young man who
seems to have no will of his own, but does
every thing that is asked of him, may be a
very good natured, but he is a very silly, fellow. If you are invited to drink at any man's
house, more than you think is wholesome, you
may say, "you wish you could, but that so

little makes you both drunk and sick, that you should only be bad company by doing it: of course, beg to be excused." If desired to play at cards, deeper than you would, refuse it ludicrously; tell them, "if you were sure to lose, you might possibly sit down; but that, as fortune may be favourable, you dread the thought of having too much money, ever since you found what an incumbrance it was to poor Harlequin, and therefore you are resolved never to put yourself in the way of winning more than such or such a sum a-day." This light way of declining invitations to vice and folly, is more becoming a young man, than philosophical or sententious refusals, which would only be laughed at.

When invited to dinner or supper, you must never usurp to yourself the best places, the best dishes, &c., but always decline them and offer them to others, except, indeed, you are offered any thing by a superior, when it would be a rudeness, if you liked it, not to accept it immediately, without the least apology. Thus, for example, were a superior the master of the table, to offer you a thing of which there was but one, to pass it to the person next to you, would be indirectly charging him that offered it to you, with a want of good manners and proper respect to his company; or, if you were the only stranger present, it would be a rudeness, if you would make a feint of refusing it, with the customary apology, " I cannot think of taking it from you, Sir;" or, " I am sorry to deprive you of it;" as it is supposed he is conscious of his own rank, and if he chose not to give it, would not have offered it ; your apology, therefore, in this case, is putting him

upon an equality with yourself. In like manner, it is rudeness to draw back, when requested, by a superior, to pass a door first, or to step
into a carriage before him. In short, it would
be endless to particularize all the instances, in
which a well-bred man shows his politeness, in
good company ; such as not yawning, singing,
whistling, warming his back at the fire, lounging, putting his legs upon the chairs, and the
like ; familiarities, which every man's good
sense must condemn, and good breeding abhor.

To write well and correct, and in a pleasing
style, is another part of polite education.
Every man who has the use of his eyes and
his right hand, can write whatever hand he
pleases. Nothing is so illiberal, as a school-
boy's scrawl. I would not have you learn a
stiff formal hand, like that of a schoolmaster ;
but a genteel, legible, and liberal hand, and to
be able to write quick. As to the correctness
and elegance of your writing, attention to
grammar does the one, and to the best authors
the other. Epistolary correspondence should
not be carried on in a studied or affected style ;
but the language should flow from the pen, as
naturally and as easily as it would from the
mouth. In short, a letter should be penned in
the same style as you would talk to your friend,
if he were present. All gentlemen transact-
ing business, write their names always in a
plain hand, that their signature may be so well
known as not to be easily counterfeited; and
they generally write them in a larger character than their common hand.

There is nothing that a young man, at his
first appearance in life, ought more to dread,
than having any ridicule fixed upon him. In

the estimation, even of the most rational men, it will lessen him, but ruin him with all the rest. Many a man has been undone, by a ridiculous nickname. The causes of nicknames among well-bred men, are generally the little defects in manner, air, or address. To have the appellation of ill-bred, awkward, muttering, left-legged, or any other, tacked always to your name, would injure you more than you are aware of: avoid, then, these little defects, (and they are easily avoided), and you need never fear a nickname.

There is a certain dignity that should be preserved, in all our pleasures. In love, a man may lose his heart, without losing his nose; at table, a man may have a distinguished palate, without being a glutton; he may love wine, without being a drunkard; he may game, without being a gambler; and so on. Every virtue has its kindred vice, and every pleasure its neighbouring disgrace. Temperance and moderation mark the gentleman; but excess the blackguard. Attend carefully, then, to the line that divides them; and remember, stop rather a yard short, than step an inch beyond it. Weigh the present enjoyment of your pleasures against their necessary consequences, and I will leave it to your own determination.

A gentleman has always some regard also to the *choice* of his amusements. If at cards, he will not be seen at cribbage, all fours, or putt; or, in sports of exercise, at skittles, foot ball, leap-frog, cricket, driving of coaches, &c. but will preserve a propriety in every part of his conduct; knowing that any imitation of the manners of the mob, will unavoidably stamp him with vulgarity.

Secrecy is another characteristic of good breeding. Be careful never to tell, in one company, what you see or hear in another; much less to divert the present company, at the expense of the last. Things apparently indifferent, may, when often repeated and told abroad, have much more serious consequences than imagined. In conversation, there is generally a tacit reliance, that what is said will not be repeated; and a man, though not enjoined to secrecy, will be excluded company. if found to be a tattler: besides, he will draw himself into a thousand scrapes, and every one will be afraid to speak before him.

Pulling out your watch in company, unasked, either at home or abroad, is a mark of ill breeding. If at home, it appears as if you were tired of your company, and wished them to be gone : if abroad, as if the hours dragged heavily, and you wished to be gone yourself. If you want to know the time, withdraw; besides, as the taking what is called a French leave was introduced, that, on one person's leaving the company, the rest might not be disturbed, looking at your watch does what that piece of politeness was designed to prevent : it is a kind of dictating to all present, and telling them it is time, or almost time, to break up.

Among other things, let me caution you against ever being in a hurry. A man of sense may be in haste, but he is never in a hurry; convinced that hurry is the surest way to make him do what he undertakes, ill. To be in a hurry, is a proof that the business in which we embark, is too great for us; of course, it is the mark of little minds, that are puzzled and perplexed, when they should be cool and deliberate. They wish to do every thing at once, and are thus able to do nothing. Be steady, then, in all your engagements; look round you, before you begin; and remember that you had better do half of them well, and leave the rest undone, than to do the whole indifferently.

From a kind of false modesty, most young men are apt to consider familiarity as unbecoming. Forwardness, I allow, is so; but there is a decent familiarity, that is necessary in the course of life. Mere formal visits, upon formal invitations, are not the thing; they create no connexion, nor will they prove of service to you; it is the careless and easy ingress and egress, at all hours, that secures an acquaintance to our interest, and this is acquired by a respectful familiarity, entered into without forfeiting your importance.

In acquiring new acquaintances, be careful not to neglect your old; for a slight of this kind is seldom forgiven. If you cannot be with your former acquaintance so often as you used to be, while you had no others, take care not to give them cause to think you neglect them; call upon them frequently, though you cannot stay long with them; tell them you are sorry to leave them so soon, and nothing should take you away but certain engagements to which good manners oblige you to attend; for it will be your interest to make all the friends you can, and as few enemies as possible. By friends, I would not be understood to mean confidential ones; but persons who speak of you respectfully, and who, consistent with their own interest, would wish to be of service to you, and would rather do you good than harm.

Another thing I must recommend to you, as characteristic of a polite education, and of having kept good company, is a graceful manner of conferring favours. The most obliging things may be done so awkwardly, as to offend, while the most disagreeable things may be done so agreeably, as to please.

There is a fashionable kind of small talk, which, however trifling it may be thought, has its use in mixed companies. Of course, you should endeavour to acquire it. By small talk, I mean a good deal to say on unimportant matters; for example, foods, the flavour and growth of wines, and the chit-chat of the day. Such conversation will serve to keep off serious subjects, that might sometimes create disputes. This chit chat is to be learned chiefly by frequenting the company of the ladies.

Never be witty, at the expense of any one present; nor gratify that idle inclination, which is too strong in most young men. I mean laughing at, or ridiculing the weakness or infirmities of others, by way of diverting the company, or displaying your own superiority. Most people have their weaknesses, their peculiar likings and aversions. Some cannot bear the sight of a cat; others, the smell of cheese, and so on. Were you to laugh at these men for their antipathies, or, by design or inattention, to bring them in their way, you could not insult them more. You may possibly thus gain the laugh on your side, for the present; but it will make the person, perhaps, at whose expense you are merry, your enemy, forever after; and even those who laugh with you, will, on a little reflection, fear you, and

probably despise you; whereas, to procure
what *one* likes, and to remove what the *other*
hates, would show them that they were the
objects of your attention, and possibly make
them more your friends, than much greater
services would have done. If you have wit,
use it to please, but not to hurt. You may
shine, but take care not to scorch. In short,
never seem to see the faults of others. Though
among the mass of men, there are, doubtless,
numbers of fools and knaves; yet were we to
tell every one of these we meet, that we know
them to be so, we should be in perpetual war.
I would detest the knave and pity the fool,
wherever I found him; but I would let neither
of them know, unnecessarily, that I did so; as
I would not be industrious to make myself enemies. As one must please others, then, in order to be pleased one's self, consider what is
agreeable to you, must be agreeable to them,
and conduct yourself accordingly.

Whispering, in company, is another act of
ill breeding. It seems to insinuate, either
that the persons whom we would not wish
should hear, are unworthy of our confidence,
or it may lead them to suppose we are speaking improperly of them; on both accounts,
therefore, abstain from it.

So pulling out one letter after another, and
reading them in company, or cutting and par-
ing one's nails, is unpolite and rude. It seems
to say, we are weary of the conversation, and
are in want of some amusement, to pass away
the time.

Humming a tune to ourselves, drumming
with our fingers on the table, making a noise
with our feet, and such like, are all breaches

of good manners, and indications of our contempt for the persons present; therefore, they
should not be indulged in.

Walking fast in the streets, is a mark of
vulgarity, implying hurry of business. It may
appear well in a mechanic or tradesman, but
suits ill with the character of a gentleman, or a
man of fashion.

Staring at any person you meet, full in the
face, is also an act of ill breeding: it looks as
if you saw something wonderful in his appearance, and is therefore a tacit reprehension.

Eating quick, or very slow at meals, is characteristic of the vulgar. The first infers poverty, that you have not had a good meal for
some time; the last, if abroad, that you dislike
your entertainment; if at home, that you are
rude enough to set before your friends, what
you cannot eat yourself. So, again, eating
your soup with your nose in the plate, is vulgar; it has the appearance of being used to
hard work, and of course an unsteady hand.—
If it be necessary, then, to avoid this, it is
much more so, that of smelling your meat.

Spitting on the carpet, is a nasty practice,
and shocking in a man of liberal education.*—
Were this to become general, it would be as
necessary to change the carpets, as the table-
cloths; besides, it will lead our acquaintance
to suppose that we have not been used to gen-

---

* Spitting upon a carpet, might have been
occasionally practised, in England, *in the time
of Lord Chesterfield;* though the Editor sup-
poses that he here alludes to *France.* Such a
violation of decency, is never witnessed, now,
in England, even amongst the rudest clowns.

teel furniture; for this reason, alone, if for no other, by all means avoid it.

Keep yourself free likewise from strange tricks or habits, such as thrusting out your tongue, continually snapping your fingers, rubbing your hands, sighing aloud, gaping with a noise like a country fellow that has been sleeping in a hayloft, or indeed with any noise; and many others that I have noticed before; these are imitations of the manners of the mob, and are degrading to a gentleman.

To conclude these miscellaneous directions, attend to the following remarks, as maxims of utility.

That the deepest learning, without good breeding, is unwelcome and tiresome pedantry, and of use no where but in a man's own closet; and consequently, of no use at all.

That a man, who is not perfectly well bred, is unfit for good company, and unwelcome in it; will consequently dislike it soon, afterwards renounce it, and be reduced to solitude, or, what is worse, to low and bad company.

That a man, who is not well bred, is fully as unfit for business, as for company.

RULES FOR CONVERSATION.

HAVING now given you full and sufficient instructions for making you well received in the best of companies; nothing remains but that I lay before you a few additional rules for your conduct, in such company. Many things, on this subject, I have mentioned before; but

some few matters remain to be mentioned
now.

Talk, then, frequently, but not long together, lest you tire the persons to whom you
are speaking; for few persons talk so well
upon a subject, as to keep up the attention of
their hearers for any length of time.

Avoid telling stories, in company, unless
they are very short, indeed, and very applicable to the subject you are upon: in this case
relate them in as few words as possible, without the least digression, and with some apology; as that you hate the telling of stories, but
the shortness of it induced you. If your story
has any wit in it, be particularly careful not to
laugh at it yourself. Nothing is more tiresome
and disagreeable, than a long tedious narrative. It betrays a gossiping disposition, and
great want of imagination; and nothing is
more ridiculous, than to express an approbation of your own story, by a laugh.

In relating any thing, avoid repetitions, or
very hackneyed expressions, such as *says he*,
or says she. Some people will use these so
often, as to take off the hearer's attention
from the story; as, in an organ out of tune,
one pipe shall perhaps sound the whole time
we are playing, and confuse the piece, so as
not to be understood.

Digressions, likewise, should be guarded
against. A story is always more agreeable
without them. Of this kind, are, " *The gentleman I am telling you of, is the son of Sir
Thomas—who lives in Harley street; you must
know him—his brother had a horse that won
the sweepstakes, at the last Newmarket meeting—Zounds! if you dont know him, you know*

nothing." Or, " *He was an upright tall old gentleman, who wore his own long hair : don't you recollect him?*"   All this is unnecessary; is very tiresome and provoking, and would be an excuse for a man's behaviour, if he were to leave us in the midst of our narrative.

Some people have a trick of holding the persons to whom they are speaking, by the button, or the hand, in order to be heard out ; conscious, I suppose, that their tale is tiresome.   Pray, never do this : if the person you speak to, is not as willing to hear your story, as you are to tell it, you had much better break off, in the middle ; for, if you tire him once, he will be afraid to listen to you a second time.

Others have a way of punching the person they are talking to, in the side ; and, at the end of every sentence, asking him some such questions as the following :—" Wasn't I right in that ?"   " You know I told you so :"   " What's your opinion ?" and the like ; or perhaps, they will be thrusting him, or jogging him with their elbow.   For mercy's sake, never give way to this ; it will make your company dreaded.

Long talkers are frequently apt to single out some unfortunate man present ; generally the most silent one of the company, or probably the person who sits next to him.   To this man, in a kind of half whisper, will they run on for half an hour together.   Nothing can be more ill bred.   But, if one of these unmerciful talkers, should attack you, if you wish to oblige him, I would recommend the hearing him, with patience : seem to do so, at least ; for you could not hurt him more, than to leave

him in the middle of his story, or discover any
impatience in the course of it.

Incessant talkers are very disagreeable companions. Nothing can be more rude, than to
engross the conversation to yourself, or to
take the words, as it were, out of another
man's mouth. Every man in company has an
equal claim to bear his part in the conversation:
and to deprive him of it, is not only unjust,
but a tacit declaration that he cannot speak so
well upon the subject, as yourself; you will
therefore take it up. What can be more rude?
I would as soon forgive a man that should stop
my mouth when I was gaping, as to take my
words from me while I was speaking.

You should never help out or forestall the
slow speaker, as if you alone were rich in expressions, and he were poor. You may take it
for granted, that every one is vain enough to
think he can talk well, though he may modestly deny it: helping a person, therefore,
out in his expressions, is a correction that will
stamp the corrector with impudence and ill
manners.

Those who contradict others, upon all occasions, and make every assertion a matter of
dispute, betray, by this behaviour, a want of
acquaintance with good breeding. He, therefore, who wishes to appear amiable with those
he converses with, will be cautious of such
expressions as these, " That can't be true,
Sir." " The affair is as I say." " That must
be false, Sir." " If what you say is true," &c.
You may as well tell a man he lies at once, as
thus indirectly impeach his veracity. It is
equally as rude, to be proving every trifling
assertion, with a bet or a wager. " I'll bet you

fifty of it," and so on. Make it, then, a constant rule, in matters of no great importance, complaisantly to submit your opinion to that of others; for a victory of this kind often costs a man the loss of a friend.

Giving advice, unasked, is another piece of rudeness. It is, in effect, declaring ourselves wiser than those to whom we give it; reproaching them with ignorance and inexperience. It is a freedom, that ought not to be taken with any common acquaintance; and yet there are those, who will be offended, if their advice is not taken. " Such a one," say they, " is above being advised. He scorns to listen to my advice ;" as if it were not a mark of greater arrogance, to expect every one to submit to their opinion, than for a man sometimes to follow his own. .

Surliness or moroseness, also, is incompatible with politeness. Such as, should any one say, " he was desired to present Mr. such a one's respects to you," to reply, " what the devil have I to do with his respects ?" My Lord inquired after you lately, and asked " how you did,"—to answer, " If he wishes to know, let him come and feel my pulse ;" and the like. A good deal of this is often affected ; but whether affected or natural, it is always offensive. A man of this stamp will occasionally be laughed at, as an oddity ; but, in the end, will be despised.

I should suppose it unnecessary to advise you to adapt your conversation to the company you are in. You would not surely start the same subject, and discourse of it in the same manner, with the old and with the young, with an officer, a clergyman, a philosopher, and a woman! No! your good sense will undoubtedly teach you to be serious with the serious, gay with the gay, and to trifle with the triflers.

There are certain expressions which are exceedingly rude, and yet there are people of liberal education that sometimes use them; as, "You don't understand me, sir." "It is not so." "You mistake." "You know nothing of the matter," &c. Is it not better to say, "I believe I do not express myself so as to be understood. Let us consider it again, whether we take it right or not." It is much more polite and amiable, to make some excuse for another, even in cases where he might justly be blamed, and to represent the mistake as common to both, than charge him with insensibility or incomprehension.

If any one should have promised you any thing, and not have fulfilled that promise, it would be very impolite to tell him he has forfeited his word; or if the same person should have disappointed you upon any occasion, would it not be better to say, "You were probably so much engaged, that you forgot my affair," or, "Perhaps, it slipped your memory:" rather than, "You thought no more about it," or, "You pay very little regard to your word." Expressions of this kind leave a sting behind them. They are a kind of provocation and affront, and very often bring on lasting quarrels.

Be careful not to appear dark and mysterious, lest you should be thought suspicious; than which, there cannot be a more unamiable character. If you appear mysterious and reserved, others will be truly so, with you;

and, in this case, there is an end to improvement, for you will gather no information. Be reserved, but never seem so. Depend upon it, nine in ten of every company you are in, will avail themselves of every indiscreet and unguarded expression of yours, if they can turn it to their own advantage. A prudent reserve, is therefore, commonly a virtue ; as, by an unwarrantable frankness, you may injure others, as well as yourself.

There is a fault, extremely common with some people, which I would have *you* to avoid. When their opinion is asked, upon any subject, they will give it with so apparent a diffidence and timidity, that one cannot, without the utmost pain, listen to them; especially if they are known to be men of universal knowledge. " Your lordship will pardon me," says one of this stamp, " if I should not be able to speak to the case in hand, so well as might be wished." " I'll venture to speak of this matter to the best of my poor abilities, and dulness of apprehension." " I fear I shall expose myself, but, in obedience to your lordship's commands" —and while they are making these apologies, they interrupt the business and tire the company.

Always look people in the face, when you speak to them, otherwise you will be thought conscious of some guilt; besides, you lose the opportunity of reading their countenances, from which you will much better learn the impression which your discourse makes upon them, than you possibly can, from their words; for words are at the will of every one, but the countenance is frequently involuntary.

If, when speaking to a person, you are not heard, and should be desired to repeat what you said, do not raise your voice in the repetition, lest you should be thought angry, on being obliged to repeat what you had said before : it was probably owing to the hearer's inattention.

One word only, as to swearing. Those who addict themselves to it, and interlard their discourse with oaths, can never be considered as gentlemen. They are generally people of low education, and are unwelcome in what is called good company. It is a vice that has no temptation to plead, but is, in every respect, as vulgar as it is wicked.

Never accustom yourself to scandal, nor listen to it; for though it may gratify the malevolence of some people, nine times out of ten it is attended with great disadvantages. The very persons to whom you tell it, will on reflection, entertain a mean opinion of you; and it will often bring you into very disagreeable situations. As there would be no evil speakers, if there were no evil hearers; it is in scandal, as in robbery; the receiver is as bad as the thief.

Besides, it will lead people to shun your company; supposing that you will speak ill of *them*, to the next acquaintance you meet.

Mimicry, the favourite amusement of little minds, has been ever the contempt of great ones. Never practise it yourself, nor ever encourage it in others. It is the most illiberal of all buffoonery; it is an insult on the person you mimic; and insults, I have often told you, are seldom forgiven.

Carefully avoid talking either of your own or other people's domestic concerns. By doing the one, you will be thought vain; by entering into the other, you will be considered

as officious. Talking of yourself, is an impertinence to the company: your affairs are nothing to them; besides, they cannot be kept
too secret. As to the affairs of others, what
are they to you? In talking of matters that
no way concern you, you are liable to commit
blunders; and should you touch any one in a
sore part, you may possibly lose his esteem.
Let your conversation, then, in mixed companies, always be general. Such is the natural
pride and vanity of our hearts, that they perpetually break out, even in people of the best
parts, in all the various modes and figures of
egotism.

Some, abruptly, speak advantageously of
themselves, without either pretence or provocation. They are impudent. Others proceed
more artfully, as they imagine, and forge ac-
cusations against themselves, complain of ca-
lumnies which they never heard, in order to
justify themselves, by exhibiting a catalogue
of their many virtues. They acknowledge it
may, indeed, seem odd, that they should talk
in that manner of themselves; it is what they
do not like, and what they never would have
done; no, no tortures should ever have forced
it from them, if they had not been thus unjustly and monstrously accused. But, in these
cases, justice is surely due to one's-self, as well
as to others; and, when our character is attacked, we may say, in our own justification,
what otherwise we never would have said.
This thin veil of modesty, drawn before vanity,
is much too transparent, to conceal it, even
from very moderate discernment.

The only sure way of avoiding these evils,
is, never to speak of yourself at all. But when,
historically, you are obliged to mention your-

self, take care not to drop one single word, that can directly or indirectly be construed as fishing for applause. Be your character what it may, it will be known; and nobody will take it upon your own word. Never imagine that any thing you can say yourself, will varnish your defects, or add lustre to your perfections; but, on the contrary, it may, and nine times in ten, will, make the former more glaring, and the latter more obscure. If you are silent upon your own subject, neither envy, nor indignation, nor ridicule, will obstruct or allay the applause which you may really deserve; but, if you publish your own panegyric, upon any occasion, or in any shape whatsoever, and however artfully dressed or disguised, they will all conspire against you, and you will be disappointed of the very end at which you aim.

Jokes, *bon mots*, or the little pleasantries of one company, will not often bear to be told in another. They are frequently local, and take their rise from certain circumstances; a second company may not be acquainted with these circumstances, and of course your story may be misunderstood, or want explaining; and if, after you have prefaced it with, " I will tell you a good thing," the sting should not be immediately perceived, you will appear exceedingly ridiculous, and wish you had not told it. Never, then, repeat, in one place, what you have heard in another.

Avoid, as much as you can, in mixed companies, argumentative, polemical conversations; which, though they should not, yet certainly do, indispose, for a time, the contending parties towards each other: and, if the controversy grows warm and noisy, endeavour to put an end to it, by some genteel levity or joke. I quieted such a conversation hubbub once, by representing to them, that, though I was persuaded none there present would repeat, out of company, what passed into it, yet I could not answer for the discretion of the passengers in the street, who must necessarily hear all that was said.

Acquaint yourself with the character and situations of the company you go into, before you give a loose to your tongue; for, should you enlarge on some virtue, which any one present may notoriously want; or condemn some vice, to which any of the company may be particularly addicted; they will be apt to think your reflections pointed and personal, and you will be sure to give offence. This consideration will naturally lead you not to suppose things said in general, to be levelled at you.

Low bred people, when they happen occasionally to be in good company, imagine themselves to be the subject of every separate conversation. If any part of the company whispers, it is about them; if they laugh, it is at them; and if any thing is said which they do not comprehend, they immediately suppose it is meant of them. This mistake is admirably ridiculed in one of our celebrated comedies: " I am sure," says Scrub, " they were talking of me, for they laughed consumedly." Now, a well bred person never thinks himself disesteemed by the company, or laughed at, unless their reflections are so gross, that he cannot be supposed to mistake them, and his honour obliges him to resent it in a proper manner. However, be assured, gentlemen never laugh at or ridicule one another, unless they are in joke, or on a footing of the greatest intimacy. If such a thing should happen once in an age, from some pert coxcomb, or some flippant woman, it is best not to seem to know it, than make the least reply.

It is a piece of politeness not to interrupt a person in a story, whether you have heard it before or not. Some are fond of telling a story, because they think they tell it well; others pride themselves in being the first teller of it; and others are pleased at being thought entrusted with it. Now, all these persons you would disappoint by answering yes; therefore, as I have told you before, that the greatest proof of politeness is to make every body happy about you, I would never deprive a person of any secret satisfaction of this sort, when I could gratify him by a minute's attention.

Be not ashamed of asking questions, if such questions lead to information : always accompany them with some excuse, and you never will be reckoned impertinent. But abrupt questions, without some apology, by all means avoid, as they imply design. There is a way of fishing for facts, which, if done judiciously, will answer every purpose; such as, taking things you wish to know, for granted. This will perhaps lead some officious person to set you right. So, again, by saying, you have heard so and so : and sometimes seeming to know more than you do, you will often get at information which you would lose by direct questions, as these would put people upon their guard, and frequently defeat the very end at which you aim.

Make it a rule never to reflect upon any body of people, for, by this means you will create a number of enemies. There are good and bad of all professions, lawyers, soldiers, parsons, or citizens. These are all men, subject to the same passions, differing only in their manner, according to the way in which they have been bred. For this reason, it is unjust as well as indiscreet, to attack them as a *corps* collectively. Many a young man has thought himself extremely clever, in abusing the clergy. What are the clergy, more than other men? Can you suppose a black gown can make any alteration in his nature? Fie, fie! think seriously, and I am convinced you will never do it. All general reflections, upon nations and societies, are the trite, thread bare jokes, of those who set up for wit, without having any, and so have recourse to commonplace. Judge of individuals, from your own knowledge of them, and not from their sex, profession, or denomination.

But, above all, let no example, no fashion, no witticism, no foolish desire of rising above what knaves call prejudices, tempt you to excuse, extenuate, or ridicule, the least breach of morality; but, upon every occasion, show the greatest abhorrence of such proceedings, and hold virtue and religion in the highest veneration.

Vulgarism in language is the next, and distinguishing characteristic of bad company, and a bad education. A man of fashion avoids nothing with more care, than that. Proverbial expressions, and trite sayings, are the flowers of the rhetoric of a vulgar man. Would he say, that men differ in their tastes; he both supports and adorns that opinion, by the good old saying, as he respectfully calls it, that "What is one man's meat, is another man's poison." If any body attempts being "smart," as he calls it, upon him; he gives him "tit for tat—aye, that he does." He has always some favourite word, for the time being; which, for the sake of using often, he commonly abuses. Such as vastly angry, vastly kind, vastly handsome, and vastly ugly. He sometimes affects hard words, by way of ornament, which he always mangles. A man of fashion never has recourse to proverbs, and vulgar aphorisms; uses neither favourite words, nor hard words; but takes great care to speak very correctly and grammatically, and to pronounce properly; that is, according to the usage of the best companies.

The conversation of the ignorant, is no conversation, and gives even them no pleasure: they tire of their own sterility, and have not matter enough to furnish them with words, to keep up a conversation.

Let me, therefore, most earnestly recommend to you, to hoard up, while you can, a great stock of knowledge; for though, during the period of youth, you may not have occasion to spend much of it; yet you may depend upon it, that a time will come, when you will want it to maintain you. Public granaries are filled in plentiful years; not that it is known, that the next, or the second, or the third year, will prove a scarce one; but because it is known, that sooner or later, such a year will come, in which the grain will be wanted. I am far from meaning, that you should always be talking wisely, in company, of books, history, and matters of knowledge. There are many companies which you will, and ought to keep, where such conversation would be misplaced and ill-timed; your own good sense must distinguish the company and time.— You must trifle with triflers; and be serious only with the serious; but dance to those who pipe. *Cur in theatrum Cato severè venisti ?*[*] was justly said to an old man: how much more so would it be, to one of your age? From the moment that you are dressed, and go out, pocket all your knowledge with your watch, and never pull it out in company, unless desired: the producing of the one unasked, implies that you are weary of the company; and the producing of the other unrequired, will make the company weary of you. Company is a republic too jealous of its liberties, to suffer a dictator, even for a quarter of an hour; and yet in that, as in all republics, there are some who really govern; but then it is by seeming to disclaim, instead of attempting to usurp the power: that is the occasion in which manners, dexterity, address, and the undefinable *je ne sçais quoi*[†] triumph. If properly exerted, their conquest is sure, and the more lasting, for not being perceived.

You are not to forget that even trifles elegantly expressed, well looked, and accompanied with graceful action, will ever please, beyond all the home-spun, unadorned sense, in the world. Reflect, on one side, how you feel within yourself, while you are forced to suffer the tedious, muddy, and ill-turned narration of some awkward fellow, even though the fact may be interesting; and on the other hand,

---

[*] Why, Cato, have you come, with this gravity, into a theatre?

[†] I know not what.

with what pleasure you attend to the relation
of a much less interesting matter, when elegantly expressed, genteelly turned, and gracefully delivered. By attending carefully to all
these *agrémens** in your daily conversation,
they will become habitual.

PEDANTRY.

Every excellence, and every virtue, has its
kindred vice or weakness; and, if carried beyond certain bounds, sinks into the one or the
other. Generosity often runs into profusion.
economy into avarice, courage into rashness,
caution into timidity, and so on:—insomuch,
that, I believe, there is more judgment re-
quired for the proper conduct of our virtues.
than for avoiding their opposite vices. Vice,
in its true light, is so deformed, that it shocks
us, at first sight; and would hardly ever seduce
us, if it did not, at first sight, wear the mask of
some virtue. But virtue is, in itself, so beautiful.
that it charms us at first; engages us more and
more, upon further acquaintance; and, as with
other beauties, we think excess impossible : it
is here, that judgment is necessary, to moderate and direct the effects of an excellent
cause. I shall apply this reasoning, at present, not to any particular virtue, but to an excellence, which, for want of judgment, is often
the cause of ridiculous and blameable effects;
I mean great learning, which, if not accompanied with sound judgment, frequently carries
us into error, pedantry, and pride.

---

† Preferences.

Some learned men, proud of their knowledge, speak only to decide, and give judgment without appeal. The consequence of which is, that mankind, provoked by the insult, and injured by the oppression, revolt; and, in order to shake off the tyranny, even call the lawful authority in question. The more you know, the more modest you should be; and (by the way) that modesty is the surest way to eminence: If you would convince others, be open to conviction yourself.

There is another species of learned men, who, though less dogmatical and supercilious, are not less impertinent. These are the communicative and shining pedants, who adorn their conversation, even with women, by happy quotations of Greek and Latin; and who have contracted such a familiarity with the Greek and Roman authors, that they call them by certain names or epithets, denoting intimacy;—as, old Homer; that sly rogue Horace; Maro, instead of Virgil; and Naso, instead of Ovid. These are often imitated by coxcombs, who have no learning at all, but who have got some names, and some scraps of ancient authors, by heart, which they improperly and impertinently retail in all companies, in hopes of passing for scholars. If, therefore, you would avoid the accusation of pedantry, on one hand, or the suspicion of ignorance, on the other, abstain from learned ostentation. Speak the language of the company you are in; speak it purely, and unlarded with any other. Never seem wiser, nor more learned, than the people you are with. Wear your learning, like your watch, in a private pocket; and do not pull it out, and strike it, merely to show that you

I

have one. If you are asked what o'clock it is, tell it; but do not proclaim it hourly and unasked, like the watchman.

Upon the whole, remember that learning (1 mean Greek and Roman learning) is a most useful and necessary ornament; of which, it is shameful not to be master; but, at the same time, most carefully avoid those errors and abuses which I have mentioned, and which too often attend it. Remember, too, that great modern knowledge is still more necessary than ancient; and that you had better know perfectly the present, than the old state of Europe; though I would have you well acquainted with both.

But, to conclude—all the above mentioned rules, however carefully you may observe. them, will lose half their effect, if unaccompanied by the Graces. Whatever you say, if you say it with a supercilious, cynical face, or an embarrassed countenance, or a silly disconcerted grin, it will be ill received. If, moreover, you mutter it, or utter it indistinctly; and ungracefully, it will be still worse received. If your air and address be vulgar, awkward, and *gauché*,* you may be esteemed indeed, if you have great intrinsic merit; but you will never please; and, without pleasing, you will rise but heavily.

---

* Left-handed—ridiculous.

MISCELLANEOUS OBSERVATIONS AND MAXIMS.

VERY few, scarcely any, are wanting in the respect which they should show to those whom they acknowledge to be infinitely their superiors; such as crowned heads, princes, and public persons of distinguished and eminent posts. It is the manner of showing that respect, which is different. The man of fashion, and of the world, expresses it in its fullest extent; but naturally, easily, and without concern: whereas, a man who is not used to keep good company, expresses it awkwardly; one sees that he is not used to it, and that it costs him a great deal; but I never saw the worst bred man living, guilty of lolling, whistling, scratching his head, and such like indecencies, in company that he respected. In such companies, therefore, the only point to be attended to is, to show that respect, which every body means to show, in an easy, unembarrassed, and graceful manner. This is what observation and experience must teach you.

Good sense bids one be civil, and endeavour to please; though nothing but experience and observation can teach one the means properly adapted to time, place, and persons.

My wishes, and my plan, were to make you shine, and distinguish yourself equally in the learned and the polite world. Few have been able to do it. Deep learning is generally tainted with pedantry, or at least unadorned by manners; as, on the other hand, polite manners, and the turn of the world, are too often unsupported by knowledge, and consequently end contemptibly, in the frivolous dissipation of drawing-rooms and *ruelles*.

Take this maxim, for an undoubted truth, that no young man can possibly improve in any company for which he has not respect enough to be under some degree of restraint.

One of the most important points of life, is decency; which is to do what is proper, and where it is proper; for many things are proper, at one time, and in one place, that are extremely improper in another. Read men, therefore, yourself, not in books, but in nature. Adopt no systems, but study them yourself.— Observe their weaknesses, their passions, their humours; of all of which, their understandings are, nine times in ten, the dupes.

If you would particularly gain the affection and friendship of particular people, whether men or women, do justice to what you find out to be their predominant excellence, if they have one; and be tender to their prevailing weakness, which every body has, unless it is of the nature of vice, or you can mend them by reproof.

Aim at perfection, in every thing, though in most things it is unattainable; however, those who aim at it, and persevere, will come much nearer to it, than those whose laziness and despondency make them abandon it, as unattainable. A man who sets out in the world with real timidity and diffidence, has not an equal chance in it; he will be discouraged, put by, or trampled upon. But, to succeed, a man, especially a young one, should have inward firmness, steadiness, and intrepidity; with exterior modesty and diffidence. He must modestly, but resolutely, assert his own rights and privi-

leges. *Suaviter in modo*, but *fortiter in re*.
He should have an apparent frankness and
openness, but with inward caution and close-
ness.

I would not have you be a valetudinarian. I
must tell you, that the best and most robust
health requires some degree of attention to
preserve. Young fellows, thinking they have
so much health and time before them, are very
apt to neglect or lavish both, and beggar themselves before they are aware : whereas, a prudent economy, in both, would make them rich
indeed; and so far from breaking in upon their
pleasures, would improve, and almost perpetu-
ate them. Be you wiser; and, before it is too
late, manage both, with frugality and care ;
and lay out neither, but upon good interest
and security.

It is always right to be prepared for all
events, the worst as well as the best : it prevents hurry and surprise, two dangerous situations in business : for I know no one thing so
useful, so necessary, in all business, as great
coolness and steadiness ; they give an incredible advantage over every person with whom
one has any transaction. Little things are not
to be neglected; for the very best things receive some addition, by a genteel and graceful
manner of doing them.

Common sense (which, in truth, is very
uncommon) is the best sense I know of; abide
by it, it will counsel you best. Read and hear,
for your amusement, ingenious systems, nice
questions, subtilly agitated, with all the re-
finements that warm imaginations suggest ;
but consider them only as exercitations for the
mind, and return always to settle with common
sense.

Mankind will sooner forgive an injury, than an insult. Some men are more captious than others ; some are always wrong-headed ; but every man living has such a share of vanity, as to be hurt by marks of slight and contempt. Every man does not pretend to be a poet, a mathematician or a statesman, and considered as such ; but every man pretends to common sense, and to fill his place in the world with common decency ; and, consequently, does not easily forgive those negligences, inattentions, and slights, which seem to call in question, or utterly deny him both these pretensions. Few will bear to be told their weaknesses. I had a very worthy friend, with whom I was intimate enough to tell him his faults ; he had but few ; I told him of them, he took it kindly of me, and corrected them. But then, he had some weaknesses that I could never tell him of directly, and of which he was so little sensible himself, that hints concerning them were lost upon him. He had a scrag neck of about a yard long ; notwithstanding which, bags being in fashion, he would wear one to his wig, and did so ; but never behind him, for, upon every motion of his head, his bag came forwards over one shoulder or the other. He took it into his head, too, that he must, occasionally, dance minuets, because other people did ; and he did so, not only extremely ill, but so awkward, so disjointed, so slim, so meagre was his figure, that, had he danced as well as ever Marcel did, it would have been ridiculous in him to have danced at all. I hinted these things to him, as plainly as friendship would allow, and to no purpose ; but to have told him the whole, so as to cure him, I must have been his father.

A proper secrecy is the only mystery of able-men : mystery is the only secrecy of weak and cunning ones.

A man who tells nothing, or who tells all, will equally have nothing told him.

If a fool knows a secret, he tells it, because he is a fool : if a knave knows one, he tells it wherever it is his interest to tell it. Others are very apt to tell what secrets they know, from the vanity of having been trusted. Trust none of these, whenever you can help it.

Inattention to the present business, be it what it will; the doing one thing, and thinking at the same time of another; or the attempting to do two things at once ; are the never failing signs of a little, frivolous mind.

Distrust all those who love you extremely upon a very slight acquaintance, and without any visible reason. Be upon your guard, too, against those who confess, as their weaknesses, all the cardinal virtues.

In your friendships, and in your enmities, let your confidence and your hostilities have certain bounds : make not the former dangerous, nor the latter irreconcileable. There are strange vicissitudes in business !

Smooth your way to the head, through the heart. The way of reason is a good one ; but it is commonly something longer, and perhaps not so sure.

Spirit is now a very fashionable word : to act with spirit, to speak with spirit, means only, to act rashly, and to talk indiscreetly. An able man shows his spirit by gentle words, and resolute actions : he is neither hot nor timid.

Never apply for what you see very little probability of obtaining. By asking improper and

unattainable things, you will accustom the ministers to refuse you so often, that they will
find it easy to refuse you the most proper and
reasonable favours. It is a common, but a most
mistaken rule, at court, to ask for every thing,
in order to get something : you do get something by it, it is true, but it is refusals and ridicule.

One good patron, at court, may be sufficient, provided you have no personal enemies ;
and, in order to have none, you must sacrifice
(as the Indians do to the devil) most of your
passions, and much of your time, to the num-
berless evil beings, that infest it ; in order to
prevent and avert the mischiefs they can do
you.

A young man, be his merit what it will, can
never raise himself; but must, like the ivy
round the oak, twine himself round some man
of great power and interest.

As kings are begotten and born like other men,
it is to be presumed that they are of the human
species ; and, perhaps, had they the same education, they might prove like other men. But,
flattered from their cradles, their hearts are
corrupted, and their heads are turned, so that
they seem to be a species by themselves. No
king ever said to himself, *homo sum, nihil hu-
mani a me alienum puto.*[*] Flattery cannot be
too strong for them ; drunk with it from their
infancy, like old drinkers, they require drams.
They prefer a personal attachment, to a public
service, and reward it better. They are vain
and weak enough to look upon it as a free will

---

[*] I am a man, and consider nothing foreign
to me, that relates to man.

offering to their merit, and not as a burnt sacrifice to their power.

Take care always to form your establishment so much within your income, as to leave a sufficient fund for unexpected contingencies, and a prudent liberality.

There is hardly a year, in any man's life, in which a small sum of ready money may not be employed to great advantage.

Among people used to affairs of moment, secrecy is much less uncommon, than is generally believed.

The greatest evils are not arrived at their utmost period, until those who are in power have lost all sense of shame. At such a time, those who should obey shake off all respect and subordination. Then is lethargic indolence roused ; but roused by convulsions.

Timorous minds are much more inclined to deliberate than to resolve.

It is more difficult for the member of a faction to live with those of his own party, than to act against those who oppose it.

A CHAPTER ADDRESSED TO AMERICANS.

THE foregoing instructions were originally written for the improvement of a European. The editor of this work takes the liberty of adding a few remarks, addressed particularly to the young gentlemen of the United States.

As there is no nation, that does not exhibit something peculiar in its manners, worthy of commendation;—so, there is none, in which something peculiar cannot be observed, that

demands reproof.—Should an American gentleman, during a visit to Europe, be seen
chewing tobacco, it matters not what may be
his dress, or his letters of introduction; he
will immediately be set down as a low bred
mechanic, or at best, as the master of a merchant vessel. No gentleman, in Europe, even
smokes, except it be occasionally, by way of
frolic; but no person, except one of the very
lowest of the working classes, is ever seen to
chew.

The practice of chewing leads to that most
ungentlemanly and abominable habit, of spitting upon the floor, and into the fire. No
floor, in the United States, however clean, no
carpet, however beautiful and costly, no fire-
grate, however bright,—not even our places of
divine worship,—are free from this detestable
pollution. A person who is guilty of so unpardonable a violation of decorum, and out-
rage against the decencies of polished life,
should be excluded from the parlour, and allowed to approach no nearer than the hall-
door steps. When in a house, and a person
has occasion to spit, it should be into one's
pocket-handkerchief; but never upon the floor,
or into the fire. The meanest and the rudest
clown in Europe, is never known to be guilty
of such an indecorum; and such a thing as a
spitting-box, is never seen there, except in a
common tavern.

There is another habit, peculiar to the
United States, and from which even some fe-
males, who class themselves as ladies, are not
entirely free,—that of lolling back, balanced,
upon the two hind legs of a chair. Such a
breach of good breeding, is never committed

in Europe. Lolling is carried even so far in America, that it is not uncommon to see attorneys lay their feet upon the council table; and the clerks and judges, theirs also upon their desks, in open court. But, low bred and disgusting as is this practice, in a court of justice, how much more reprehensible is it, in places of a still greater solemnity of character: how must the feelings of a truly religious and devout man, be wounded, when he sees the legs extended, in the same indecent posture, in the house of God!

Another violation of decorum, confined chiefly to taverns and boarding-houses of an ordinary class, is that of reaching across a table, or across three or four persons sitting next to him who wishes for some particular dish. This is not only vulgar, but inconvenient. It is a sure sign of having been accustomed to low company; and should be avoided, by every one who is ambitious of being thought a gentleman. The nasty practice of carving with one's own knife and fork, and of using one's own knife or spoon when wanting salt or sugar, does not call less loudly for amendment; but cannot always be dispensed with, unless the mistress of the house will be careful in performing her duty, by seeing that the table is fully provided with such things as a decent table requires.

DR. WATTS'

ADVICE

TO A

YOUNG MAN

ON HIS

ENTRANCE INTO THE WORLD.

———

Curino was a young man, brought up to a reputable trade; the term of his apprenticeship was almost expired, and he was contriving how he might venture into the world with safety, and pursue business with innocence and success. Among his near kindred, *Serenus* was one, a gentleman of considerable character in the sacred profession; and after he had consulted with his father, who was a merchant of great esteem and experience, he also thought fit to seek a word of advice from the divine. *Serenus* had such a respect for his young kinsman, that he set his thoughts at work on this subject, and with some tender expressions, which melted the youth into tears, he put into his hand a paper of his best counsels. *Curino* entered upon business, pursued his employment with uncommon advantage, and under the blessing of heaven advanced himself to a considerable estate. He lived with honour in the world, and gave a lustre to the religion which he professed: and after a long life of piety and usefulness, he died with a sacred composure of soul under the influences of Christian hope. Some of his neighbours wondered at his felicity in this world, joined with so much innocence, and such severe virtue. But after his death, this paper was found in his closet, which was drawn up by his kinsman in holy orders, and was supposed to have had a large share in procuring his happiness.

ADVICE TO A YOUNG MAN.

RULE I.

Kinsman, I presume you desire to be happy here and hereafter; you know there are a thousand difficulties which attend this pursuit, some of them perhaps you foresee, but there are multitudes which you could never think of. Never trust therefore to *your own understanding* in the things of this world, where you can have the advice of a *wise and faithful friend;* nor dare venture the more important concerns of your soul and your eternal interests in the world to come, upon the mere *light of nature,* and the *dictates of your own reason;* since the *word of God,* and the advice of Heaven, lie in your hands. Vain and thoughtless indeed are those children of pride, who choose to turn heathens in the midst of Great Britain; who live upon the mere religion of nature and their own stock, when they have been trained up among all the superior advantages of *Christianity*, and the blessings of divine revelation and grace.

RULE II.

Whatsoever your circumstances may be in this world, still value your *Bible*, as your best treasure; and whatsoever be your employment here, still look upon religion as your best business. Your Bible contains eternal life in it, and all the riches of the upper world; and religion is the only way to become a possessor of them.

RULE III.

To direct your carriage toward *God*, converse particularly with the book of Psalms; *David* was a man of sincere and eminent devotion. To behave aright among *men*, acquaint yourself with the whole book of Proverbs: *Solomon* was a man of large experience and wisdom. And to perfect your directions in both these, read the Gospels and the Epistles; you will find the best of rules and the best of examples there, and those more immediately suited to the Christian life.

RULE IV.

As a *man*, maintain strict temperance and sobriety, by a wise government of your appetites and passions; as a neighbour, influence and engage all around you to be your friends, by a temper and carriage made up of prudence and goodness; and let the poor have a certain share in all your yearly profits. As a trader, keep that golden sentence of our Saviour's ever before you—" Whatever you would that men should do unto you, do you also unto them."

While you make the *precepts* of scripture the constant rule of your duty, you may with courage rest upon the *promises* of scripture as the springs of your encouragement. All divine assistances and divine recompenses are contained in them. The spirit of light and grace is promised to assist them that ask it. Heaven and glory are promised to reward the faithful and the obedient.

In every affair of life, begin with God. Consult him in every thing that concerns you. View him as the author of all your blessings and all your hopes, as your best friend and your eternal portion. Meditate on him in this view, with a continual renewal of your trust in him, and a daily surrender of yourself to him, till you feel that you love him most entirely, that you serve him with sincere delight, and that you cannot live a day without God in the world.

You know yourself to be a man, an indigent creature, and a sinner, and you profess to be a Christian, a disciple of the blessed Jesus; but never think you know Christ nor yourself, as you ought, till you find a daily need of him, for righteousness and strength, for pardon and sanctification; and let him be your constant introducer to the great God, though he sit upon a throne of grace. Remember his own words, John xiv. 6, "No man cometh to the Father but by me."

Make prayer a pleasure and not a task, and then you will not forget nor omit it. If ever you have lived in a praying family, never let it be your fault if you do not live in one always. Believe that day, that hour, or those minutes to be all wasted and lost, which any worldly pretences would tempt you to save out of the public worship of the church, the certain and constant duties of the closet, or any necessary services for God and godliness. Beware lest a blast attend it, and not a blessing. If God had not reserved one day in seven to himself, I fear religion would have been lost out of the world; and every day of the week exposed to a curse which has no morning religion.

See that you watch and labour, as well as pray. Diligence and dependance must be united in the practice of every Christian. It is the same wise man acquaints us, that "the hand of the diligent and the blessing of the Lord joined together make us rich," Prov. x. 4—22, rich in the treasures of body or mind, of time or eternity.

It is your duty, indeed, under a sense of your own weakness, to pray daily against sin; but if you would effectually avoid it, you must also avoid temptation, and every dangerous opportunity. Set a double guard, wheresoever you feel or suspect an enemy at hand—The world without and the heart within, have so much

flattery and deceit in them, that we must keep
a sharp eye upon both, lest we are trapped into
mischief between them.

RULE X.

Honour, profit, and pleasure, have been
sometimes called the world's trinity: they are
its three chief idols; each of them is sufficient
to draw a soul off from God, and ruin it for
ever. Beware of them, therefore, and of all
their subtle insinuations, if you would be innocent and happy.

Remember that the honour which comes
from God, the approbation of Heaven, and of
your own conscience, are infinitely more valuable than all the esteem or applause of men.
Dare not venture one step out of the road of
Heaven, for fear of being laughed at for walking strictly in it. It is a poor religion that
cannot stand against a jest.

Sell not your hopes of heavenly treasures,
nor any thing that belongs to your eternal interest, for any of the advantages of the present life: "What shall it profit a man, to gain
the whole world, and lose his own soul?"

Remember also the words of the wise man,
"He that loveth pleasure, shall be a poor
man;" he that indulges himself in wine and
oil, that is, in drinking, in feasting, and in
sensual gratifications, shall not be rich. It is
one of St. Paul's characters of a most degenerate age, when "men become lovers of pleasure, more than lovers of God." And that
"fleshly lusts war against the soul," is St.
Peter's caveat to the Christians of his time.

RULE XI.

Preserve your conscience always soft and sensible. If but one sin force its way into that tender part of the soul, and dwell easy there, the road is paved for a thousand iniquities.

And take heed, that under any scruple, doubt, or temptation whatsoever, you never let any reasonings satisfy your conscience, which will not be a sufficient apology to the great Judge at the last day.

RULE XII.

Keep this thought ever in your mind—it is a world of vanity and vexation in which you live; the flatteries and promises of it are vain and deceitful; prepare therefore to meet disappointments. Many of its occurrences are teasing and vexatious. In every ruffling storm without, possess your spirit in patience, and let all be calm and serene within. Clouds and tempests are only found in the lower skies; the Heavens above are ever bright and clear. Let your heart and hope dwell much in these serene regions; live as a stranger here on earth, but as a citizen of Heaven, if you will maintain a soul at ease.

RULE XIII.

Since in many things we offend all, and there is not a day passes which is perfectly free from sin, let " repentance towards God, and faith in our Lord Jesus Christ," be your daily work. A frequent renewal of these exercises, which make a Christian at first, will be a constant evidence of your sincere Christianity, and give you peace in life, and hope in death.

RULE XIV.

Ever carry about with you such a sense of the uncertainty of every thing in this life, and of life itself, as to put nothing off till to-morrow, which you can conveniently do to-day. Dilatory persons are frequently exposed to surprise and hurry in every thing that belongs to them; the time is come, and they are unprepared. Let the concerns of your soul and your shop, your trade and your religion, lie always in such order as far as possible, that death at a short warning may be no occasion for a disquieting tumult in your spirit, and that you may escape the anguish of a bitter repentance in a dying hour.

Phronimus, a considerable east-land merchant, happened to meet with a copy of these Rules about the time he permitted his son to commence partnership with him in his trade; he transcribed them with his own hand, and made a present of them to the youth, together with the articles of partnership. Here, young man, said he, is a paper of more worth than these articles. Read it over once a month, till it is wrought in your soul and temper. Walk by these rules, and I can trust my estate in your hands. Copy out these counsels in your life, and you will make me and yourself easy and happy.

TEN PRECEPTS,

WILLIAM LORD BURGHLEY,

Lord-High-Treasurer of England,

TO HIS SON

ROBERT CECIL,

Afterwards the Earl of Salisbury.

———

SON ROBERT,

The virtuous inclination of thy matchless
mother, by whose tender and godly care thy
infancy was governed, together with thy education under so zealous and excellent a tutor,
puts me in rather assurance than hope, that
you are not ignorant of that *summum bonum*,
which is only able to make thee happy as well
in thy death as life; I mean, the true knowledge and worship of thy Creator and Re-
deemer, without which all other things are
vain and miserable: so that, thy youth being
guided by so sufficient a teacher, I make no
doubt but he will furnish thy life with divine
and moral documents. Yet, that I may not
cast off the care beseeming a parent towards
his child, or that thou shouldest have cause to

derive thy whole felicity and welfare rather from others than whence thou receivedst thy breath and being, I think it fit and agreeable to the affection I bear thee, to help thee with such rules and advertisements for the squaring of thy life, as are rather gained by experience than by much reading; to the end that, entering into this exorbitant age, thou mayest be the better prepared to shun those scandalous courses whereunto the world, and the lack of experience, may easily draw thee. And, because I will not confound thy memory, I have reduced them into ten precepts; and, next unto Moses's tables, if thou imprint them in thy mind, thou shalt reap the benefit, and I the content. And they are these following.

I.

When it shall please God to bring thee to man's estate, use great providence and circumspection in choosing thy wife; for thence will spring all thy future good or evil: and it is an action of life, like unto a stratagem of war, wherein a man can err but once. If thy estate be good, match near home and at leisure; if weak, far off and quickly. Inquire diligently of her disposition, and how her parents have been inclined in their youth. Let her not be poor, how generous soever; for a man can buy nothing in the market with gentility. Nor choose a base and uncomely creature altogether for wealth; for it will cause contempt in others, and loathing in thee. Neither make choice of a dwarf or a fool; for by the one thou shalt beget a race of pigmies, the other will be thy continual disgrace; and it will yerke thee to hear her talk: for thou shalt find it to thy great grief, that there is nothing more fulsome than a she-fool.

And, touching the guiding of thy house, let thy hospitality be moderate; and, according to the means of thy estate, rather plentiful than sparing, but not costly; for I never knew any man grow poor by keeping an orderly table. But some consume themselves through secret vices, and their hospitality bears the blame. But banish swinish drunkards out of thine house, which is a vice impairing health, consuming much, and makes no show. I never heard praise ascribed to the drunkard, but for the well-bearing of his drink; which is a better commendation for a brewer's horse or a drayman, than for either a gentleman or a serving man. Beware thou spend not above three or four parts of thy revenues, nor above a third part of that in thy house; for the other two parts will do no more than defray the extraordinaries, which always surmount the ordinary by much: otherwise thou shalt live, like a rich beggar, in continual want. And the needy man can never live happily nor contentedly; for every disaster makes him ready to mortgage or sell; and that gentleman who sells an acre of land, sells an ounce of credit: for gentility is nothing else but ancient riches; so that if the foundation shall at any time sink, the building must need follow.—So much for the first precept.

II.

Bring thy children up in learning and obedience, yet without outward austerity. Praise them openly, reprehend them secretly. Give them good countenance and convenient main-

tenance according to thy ability, otherwise thy
life would seem their bondage; and what portion thou shalt leave them at thy death, they
will thank death for it, and not thee. And I
am persuaded that the foolish cockering of
some parents, and the over-stern carriage of
others, causeth more men and women to take
ill courses, than their own vicious inclinations.
Marry thy daughters in time, lest they marry
themselves. And suffer not thy sons to pass
the Alps; for they shall learn nothing there
but pride, blasphemy, and atheism; and if by
travel they get a few broken languages, that
shall profit them nothing more than to have
one meat served in divers dishes. Neither, by
my consent, shalt thou train them up in wars;
for he that sets up his rest to live by that profession, can hardly be an honest man or a good
Christian: beside, it is a science no longer in
request than use; for, soldiers in peace are
like chimneys in summer.

III.

Live not in the country without corn and
cattle about thee; for he that putteth his hand
to the purse for every expense of household,
is like him that keepeth water in a sieve: and
what provision thou shalt want, learn to buy it
at the best hand; for there is one penny saved
in four, betwixt buying in thy need, and when
the markets and seasons serve fittest for it. Be
not served with kinsmen, or friends, or men en-
treated to stay; for they expect much and do
little: nor with such as are amorous; for their
heads are intoxicated. And keep rather too
few, than one too many. Feed them well, and
pay them with the most; and then thou mayest
boldly require service at their hands.

IV.

Let thy kindred and allies be welcome to thy house and table. Grace them with thy countenance, and further them in all honest actions; for by these means thou shalt so double the band of nature, as thou shalt find them so many advocates to plead an apology for thee behind thy back. But shake off those glow-worms, I mean parasites and sycophants, who will feed and fawn upon thee in the summer of prosperity; but, in adverse storms, they will shelter thee no more than an arbour in winter.

V.

Beware of suretyship for thy best friends. He that payeth another man's debts, seeketh his own decay. But if thou canst not otherwise choose, rather lend thy money thyself upon good bonds, although thou borrow it; so shalt thou secure thyself and pleasure thy friend. Neither borrow money of a neighbour or a friend, but of a stranger; where, paying for it, thou shalt hear no more of it; otherwise thou shalt eclipse thy credit, lose thy freedom, and pay as dear as to another. But in borrowing of money, be precious of thy word; for he that hath care of keeping days of payment, is lord of another man's purse.

VI.

Undertake no suit against a poor man with receiving much wrong; for, besides that thou makest him thy compeer, it is a base conquest to triumph where there is small resistance. Neither attempt law against any man before thou be fully resolved that thou hast right on thy side, and then spare not for either money or pains; for, a cause or two so followed and obtained, will free thee from suits great part of thy life.

VII.

Be sure to keep some great man thy friend; but trouble him not for trifles. Compliment him often with many, yet small, gifts, and of little charge. And if thou hast cause to bestow any great gratuity, let it be something which may be daily in sight; otherwise, in this ambitious age, thou shalt remain like a hop without a pole, live in obscurity, and be made a foot-ball for every insulting companion to spurn at.

VIII.

Towards thy superiors, be humble, yet generous: with thine equals, familiar, yet respective. Towards thine inferiors show much humanity, and some familiarity; as to bow the body, stretch forth the hand, and to uncover the head, with such like popular compliments. The first prepares thy way to advancement: the second makes thee known for a man well bred: the third gains a good report, which, once got, is easily kept; for right humanity takes such deep root in the minds of the multitude, as they are easilier gained by unprofitable courtesies than by churlish benefits. Yet I advise thee not to affect or neglect popularity too much. Seek not to be Essex: shun to be Raleigh.

IX.

Trust not any man with thy life, credit, or estate; for it is mere folly for a man to enthrall

K

himself to a friend, as though, occasion being offered, he should not dare to become thy enemy.

X.

Be not scurrilous in conversation, nor satirical in thy jests; the one will make thee unwelcome to all company, the other pulls on quarrels, and gets the hatred of thy best friends; for suspicious jests (when any of them savour of truth) leave a bitterness in the minds of those which are touched. And, albeit I have already pointed at this inclusively, yet I think it necessary to leave it thee as a special caution; because I have seen many so prone to quip and gird, as they would rather lose their friend than their jest. And, if perchance their boiling brain yield a quaint scoff, they will travail to be delivered of it as a woman with child. These nimble fancies are but the froth of wit.

THE

HONOURS OF THE TABLE,

OR,

RULES

FOR

BEHAVIOUR DURING MEALS;

WITH THE

WHOLE ART OF CARVING,

Illustrated with a variety of Cuts.

———

PHILADELPHIA:

PUBLISHED BY JOHN GRIGG,

No. 9, North Fourth Street.

Clark & Raser, Printers, 33 *Carter's Alley.*

1827.

THE

Honours of the Table.

RULES FOR BEHAVIOUR AT TABLE.

OF all the graceful accomplishments, and of every branch of polite education, it has been long admitted, that a gentleman and lady never show themselves to more advantage, than in acquitting themselves well in the honours of the table; that is to say, in serving their guests and treating their friends, agreeable to their rank and situation in life.

Next to giving them a good dinner, is treating them with hospitality and attention, and this attention is what young people have to learn. Experience will teach them, in time, but till they learn, they will always appear ungraceful and awkward.

In all public companies precedence is attended to, and particularly at table. Women have here always taken place of men, and both men and women have sat above each other, according to the rank they bear in life. Where a company is equal in point of rank, married ladies take place of single ones, and older ones of younger ones.

When dinner is announced, the mistress of the house requests the lady first in rank, in company, to show the way to the rest, and walk first into the room where the table is

served; she then asks the second in precedence to follow, and after all the ladies are
passed, she brings up the rear herself.—The
master of the house does the same with the
gentlemen. Among persons of real distinction, this marshalling of the company is unnecessary, every woman and every man present
knows his rank and precedence, and takes his
lead, without any direction from the mistress
or the master.

When they enter the dining-room, each
takes his place in the same order: the mistress of the table sits at the upper end, those
of superior rank next her, right and left, those
next in rank following, then the gentlemen,
and the master at the lower end; and nothing
is considered as a greater mark of ill breeding,
than for a person to interrupt this order, or
seat himself higher than he ought. Custom,
however, has lately introduced a new mode of
seating. A gentleman and a lady sitting al-
ternately round the table, and this, for the
better convenience of a lady's being attended
to, and served by the gentleman next her. But
notwithstanding this promiscuous seating, the
ladies, whether above or below, are to be
served in order, according to their rank or
age; after them the gentlemen, in the same
manner.

The mistress of the house always sits at the
upper end of her table, provided any ladies are
present; and her husband at the lower end;
but, if the company consist of gentlemen only,
the mistress seldom appears; in which case, the
master takes the upper seat. *Note.* At whatever part of the table the mistress of the house
sits, that will ever be considered as the first
place.

As eating a great deal is deemed indelicate in a lady, (for her character should be rather divine than sensual,) it will be ill manners to help her to a large slice of meat at once, or fill her plate too full. When you have served her with meat, she should be asked what kind of vegetables she likes, and the gentleman sitting next the dish that holds those vegetables, should be requested to help her.

Where there are several dishes at table, the mistress of the house carves that which is before her, and desires her husband, or the person at the bottom of the table, to carve the joint or bird before *him*. Soup is generally the first thing served, and should be stirred from the bottom; fish, if there is any, the next.

But in serving their guests, the master or mistress should distribute their favours equally and as impartially as they can. I have sometimes seen a large dish of fish extend no farther than to the fifth person, when there have been ten persons, and a haunch of venison lose all its fat before half the table tasted it.

If you have a bird at table, a delicacy, which you cannot apportion out to all as you wish, cut it up and hand it round by a servant; in this case, out of modesty, persons will take but a small part, and perhaps a part which you could not send to them without disrespect. Some, in such a case, ask their guests, whether they will please to have any, and what part; and this on the same principle.

The master or mistress of the table should continue eating, whilst any of the company are so employed; and to enable themselves to do this, they should help themselves accordingly.

Where there are not two courses, but one course and a remove, that is, a dish to be brought up, when one is taken away, the mistress or person who presides, should acquaint her company with what is to come; or if the whole is put on the table at once, should tell her friends, that " they see their dinner;" but, they should be told, what wine or other liquors is on the sideboard. Sometimes a cold joint of meat, or a sallad, is placed on the side-board. In this case, it should be announced to the company.

If any of the company seem backward in asking for wine, it is the part of the master to ask or invite them to drink, or he will be thought to grudge his liquor; and it is the part of the mistress or master to ask those friends who seemed to have dined, whether they would please to have more. As it is un-seemly in ladies to call for wine, the gentle-men present should ask them in turn, whether it is agreeable to drink a glass of wine. " Mrs ———, will you do me the honour to drink a glass of wine with me?" and what kind of the wine present they prefer, and call for two glasses of such wine, accordingly. Each then waits till the other is served, when they bow to each other and drink.

Habit having made a pint of wine after din-ner almost necessary to a man who eats freely, which is not the case with women; and as their sitting and drinking with the men, would be unseemly, it is customary, after the cloth and dessert are removed, and two or three glasses of wine are gone round, for the ladies to retire and leave the men to themselves, and for this, 'tis the part of the mistress of the house to make the motion for retiring, by privately consulting the ladies present, whether they please to withdraw. The ladies thus rising, the men should rise of course, and the gentlemen next the door should open it, to let them pass.

As it is ungenteel to urge men to drink more than they like, to sing forth the praises of a bumper, or complain of the light in their glasses, so is it equally so, to eye your friend, whilst he is filling his glass, or suffer the bottle to stop when it comes to you.

RULES FOR WAITING AT TABLE.

A GOOD servant will be industrious, and attend to the following rules in waiting; but where he is remiss, it is the duty of the master or mistress to remind him.

1. If there is a soup for dinner, according to the number of the company to lay each person a flat plate, and a soup plate over it, a napkin, knife, fork, and spoon, and to place the chairs. If there is no soup, the soup-plate may be omitted.

2. To stand with his back to the sideboard, looking on the table. This is the office of the principal servant. If there are more, then to stand round the table, or, if each person's servant is present, that servant should stand behind his mistress' or master's chair.

3. To keep the dishes in order upon the table, as they were at first put on.

4. If any of the garnish of the dishes falls on the cloth, to remove it from the table in a

plate with a spoon, thus keeping the table free from litter.

5. To change each person's plate, knife, fork, and spoon, as soon as they are done with them. This will be known, by the person's putting the handles of his knife and fork into his plate.

6. To look round and see if any want bread, and help them to it, before it is called for.

7. To hand the decoraments of the table. *viz.* oil, vinegar, or mustard, to those who want, anticipating even their wishes. Every one knows with what mustard is eaten, with what vinegar, and so on; and a diligent, attentive servant, will always hand it, before it is asked for.

8. To give the plates, &c. perfectly clean and free from dust, and never give a second glass of wine, in a glass that has been once used. If there is not a sufficient change of glasses, he should have a vessel of water under the sideboard, to dip them in, and should wipe them bright.

9. It is genteel to have thin gill-glasses, and the servant should fill them only half full, this prevents spilling, and the foot of the glass should be perfectly dry, before it is given.

10. To give nothing but on a waiter, and always to hand it with the left hand, and on the left side of the person he serves. When serving wine, to put his thumb on the foot of the glass, this will prevent its overthrow.

11. Never to reach across a table, or in serving one person to put his hand or arm before another.

12. To tread lightly across the room, and never to speak, but in reply to a question asked, and then in a modest under voice.

13. When the dishes are to be removed, to remove them with care, so as not to spill the sauce or gravy over any of the company; to clean the table-cloth from crumbs, if a second course is to be served up; if not, to take away the knives, forks, and spoons, in a knife-tray, clear away the plates, take up the pieces of bread with a fork, roll up the cloth to prevent the crumbs falling on the floor, rub the table clean and bright, and put on the wine, &c. from the sideboard, with a decanter of water and plenty of clean glasses.

14. Where water glasses are used after dinner, to wash the fingers; to put on those glasses half full of clean water, when the table is cleared, but before the cloth is removed.

These things are the province of the servants, but as few servants are thorough good waiters, and as the master of the house is responsible for his attendants, it is incumbent on him to see that his company is properly served and attended. For a table ill served and attended, is always a reflection on the good conduct of the mistress or master.

Having now pointed out the duty of the person entertaining, I will say a few words to those entertained. In my *principles of politeness*, a book which has gone through a great number of editions, and of course, is very well known, I had occasion to touch upon behaviour at table; but as those few rules may not occur at this instant to every one, I trust I shall be pardoned in repeating them.

" Eating quick or very slow at meals, is characteristic of the vulgar; the first infers poverty, that you have not had a good meal

for some time; the last, if abroad, that you
dislike your entertainment; if at home, that
you are rude enough to set before your friends,
what you cannot eat yourself. So again, eating your soup with your nose in the plate is
vulgar, it has the appearance of being used to
hard work, and having of course an unsteady
hand. If it be necessary then to avoid this, it
is much more so, that of smelling to the meat
whilst on your fork, before you put it to your
mouth. I have seen an ill bred fellow do this,
and have been so angry, that I could have
kicked him from the table. If you dislike
what you have, leave it; but on no account,
by smelling to, or examining it, charge your
friend with putting unwholesome provisions
before you.

" To be well received, you must always be
circumspect at table, where it is exceedingly
rude, to scratch any part of your body, to spit,
or blow your nose, (if you can't avoid it, turn
your head,) to eat greedily, to lean your elbows on the table, to sit too far from it, to pick
your teeth before the dishes are removed, or
to leave the table before grace is said.

" Drinking of healths is now growing out of
fashion, and is very unpolite in good company.
Custom once had made it universal, but the
improved manners of the age, now render it
vulgar. What can be more rude or ridiculous,
than to interrupt persons at their meals, with
unnecessary compliments? Abstain then from
this silly custom, where you find it out of use,
and use it only at those tables, where it continues general.

" When you see but little of a thing at table,
or a viand that is scarce and dear, do not seem
covetous of it, for every one will expect a taste

of it as well as yourself; and when a bird is cut up, and served round to the company to take that part they like, it will show a becoming modesty to take the worst part.

" When invited to dinner, be always there in time; there cannot be a greater rudeness, if you are a person of any weight with your friend, than to oblige him to delay his dinner for your coming, (besides the chance of spoiling it) or more unpolite to the rest of the company, to make them wait for you. Be always there a quarter of an hour before the appointed time, and remember that punctuality in this matter, is a test of good breeding.

" If a superior, the master of the table, offers you a thing of which there is but one, to pass it to the person next you, would be indirectly charging him that offered it to you, with a want of good manners and proper respect to his company; or, if you are the only stranger present, it would be rudeness to make a feint of refusing it, with the customary apology, *I cannot think of taking it from you, sir*, or, *I am sorry to deprive you of it*, it being supposed he is conscious of his own rank, and if he chose not to give it, would not have offered it; your apology, therefore, in this case, is a rudeness, by putting him on an equality with yourself; in like manner, it would be a rudeness, to draw back, when requested by a superior to pass the door first, or step into a carriage before him.

" If a man of rank is of the party, it is a mark of respect, for the master to meet him at the coach-door and usher him in.

" In a word, when invited to dine or sup at the house of any well bred man, observe how he doth the honours of his table; mark his manner of treating his company, attend to the compliments of congratulation or condolence that he pays, and take notice of his address, to his superiors, his equals and his inferiors; nay his very looks and tone of his voice are worthy your attention, for we cannot please without a union of them all.

" Should you invite any one to dine or sup with you, recollect whether ever you had observed him to prefer one thing to another, and endeavour to procure that thing; when at table, say, *I think you seemed to give this dish a preference, I therefore ordered it. This is the wine I observed you best like, I have therefore been at some pains to procure it.* Trifling as these things may appear, they prove an attention to the person they are said to and an attention in trifles is the test of respect; the compliment will not be lost.

" If the necessities of nature oblige you at any time, (particularly at dinner,) to withdraw from the company you are in, endeavour to steal away unperceived, or make some excuse for retiring, that may keep your motives for withdrawing a secret; and on your return, be careful not to announce that return, or suffer any adjusting of your dress, or replacing of your watch, to say from whence you came. To act otherwise is indelicate and rude."

THE ART OF CARVING.

THE author of this work, from a conviction that the knowledge it communicates, is one of the accomplishments of a gentleman, and that the *Art of Carving* is little known, but to those who have long been accustomed to it, persuades himself he cannot make the rising generation a more useful or acceptable present, than to lay before them a book, that will teach them to acquit themselves well, in the discharge of this part of the honours of the table. We are always in pain for a man, who instead of cutting up a fowl genteelly, is hacking for half an hour across a bone, greasing himself, and bespatter-ing the company with the sauce; but where the master or mistress of a table, dissects a bird with ease and grace, or serves her guests with such parts as are best flavoured, and most es-teemed, they are not only well thought of, but admired. The principal things that are brought then to table are here delineated, and the cus-tomary method of carving them pointed out, in a manner that with little attention, will be readily understood, and the knowledge of carv-ing, with a little practice, easily acquired.

Young folks, unaccustomed to serving at table, will, with the help of these cuts, and the instructions accompanying them, soon be able to carve well; if at the same time they will, as occasion offers, take notice, how a good carver proceeds, when a joint or fowl is before him.

I have also taken the liberty of pointing out in the course of these instructions what parts of viands served up are most esteemed, that persons carving may be enabled to show a pro-per attention to their best guests and friends, and may help them to their liking.

There are some graceful methods of carv-ing, that should also be attended to, such as not to rise from our seat, if we can help it, but to have a seat high enough to give us a command of the table; not to help any one to too much at a time, nor to give the nice parts all to one person; but to distribute them, if

possible among the whole, or the best to
those of superior rank, in preference to those
of inferior, and not to cut the slices too thick
or too thin, and to help them to gravy, re-
moving the cold fat that swims on it, in cold
weather; but it is generally best to ask our
friends what part they like best.

We will then begin with those joints, &c.
that are simple and easy to be carved, and afterwards proceed to such as are more compli-
cate and difficult.

Leg of Mutton.

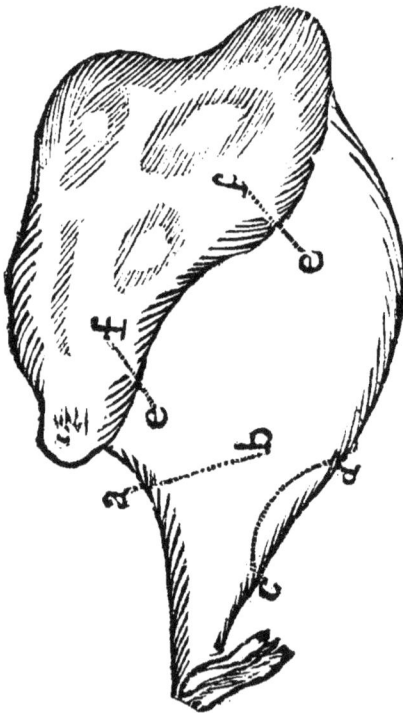

This cut represents a leg or *jigot* of boiled mutton; it should be served up in the dish as it lies, lying upon its back; but when roasted, the under side, as here represented by the letter *d*, should lie uppermost in the dish, as in a ham, (which see) and in this case, as it will be necessary occasionally to turn it so, as to get readily at the under side, and cut it in the direction of *a, b*, the shank, which is here broken and bent for the conveniency of putting it into a less pot or vessel to boil it, is not broken or bent in a roasted joint, of course, should be wound round (after it is taken off the spit,) with half a sheet of writing paper, and so sent up to table, that a person carving it may take hold of it, without greasing his hands. Accordingly when he wishes to cut it on the under side, it being too heavy a joint to be easily turned with a fork, the carver is to take hold of the shank with his left hand, and he will thus be able to turn it readily, so as to cut it where he pleases with his right.

A leg of wether mutton, which is by far the best flavoured, may be readily known when bought, by the kernel, or little round lump of fat, just above the letters *a, e*.

When a leg of mutton is first cut, the person carving, should turn the joint towards him, as it here lies, the shank to the left hand; then holding it steady with his fork, he should cut in deep on the fleshy part, in the hollow of the thigh, quite to the bone, in the direction *a, b*. Thus will he cut right through the kernel of fat, called the *Pope's eye*, which many are fond of. The most juicy parts of the leg, are in the thick part of it, from the line *a, b*, upwards, towards *e*, but many prefer the drier part, which is about the shank or knuckles; this part is by far the coarser, but as I said, some prefer it, and call it the venison part, though it is less like venison than any other part of the joint. The fat of this joint lies chiefly on the ridge e, e, and is to be cut in the direction e, f.

As many are fond of having a bone, and have an idea, that the nearer the bone, the sweeter the flesh; in a leg of mutton, there is but one bone readily to be got at, and that a small one; this is the *cramp bone*, by some called the *gentleman's bone*, and is to be cut out, by taking hold of the shank-bone with the left hand, and with a knife, cutting down to the thigh-bone at the point d, then passing the knife under the cramp-bone, in the direction d, c, it may easily be cut out.

Shoulder of Mutton.

Figure 1, represents a shoulder of mutton, which is sometimes salted and boiled by fanciful people; but customarily served up roasted, and laid in a dish, with the back or upper side uppermost, as here represented.

When not over-roasted it is a joint very full of gravy, much more so than a leg, and as such, by many preferred, and particularly as having many very good, delicate, and savoury parts in it.

The shank-bone should be wound round with writing paper, as pointed out in the leg, that the person carving may take hold of it, to turn it as he wishes. Now, when it is first cut, it should be in the hollow part of it, in the direction a, b, and the knife should be passed deep to the bone. The gravy then runs fast into the dish, and the part cut, opens wide enough to take many slices from it readily.

A Shoulder of Mutton.—No. 1.

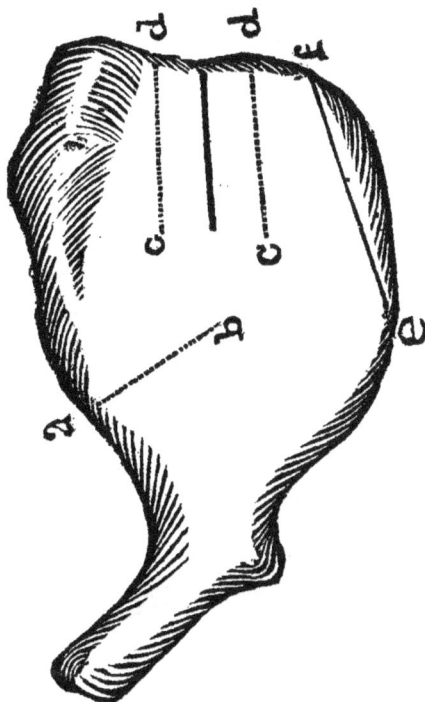

The best fat, that which is full of kernels and best flavoured, lies on the outer edge, and is to be cut out in thin slices in the direction *e, f*. If many are at table, and the hollow part cut in the line *a, b*, is all eaten, some very good and delicate slices may be cut out on each side of the ridge of the blade-bone, in the direction *c, d*. The line between these two dotted lines, is that in the direction of which the edge or ridge of the blade-bone lies, and cannot be cut across.

A Shoulder of Mutton.—No. 2.

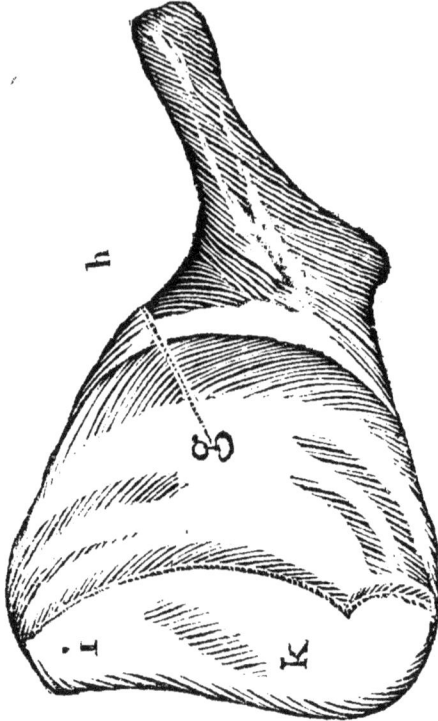

On the under side of the shoulder, as represented in figure 2, there are two parts, very full of gravy, and such as many persons prefer to those of the upper side. One is a deep cut, in the direction *g, h,* accompanied with fat, and the other all lean, in a line from *i* to *k*.

The parts about the shank are coarse and dry, as about the knuckle in the leg; but yet some prefer this dry part, as being less rich or luscious, and of course, less apt to cloy.

A shoulder of mutton over-roasted is spoiled.

A Leg of Pork.

Whether boiled or roasted, is sent up to table as a leg of mutton roasted, and cut up in the same manner; of course, I shall refer you to what I have said on that joint, only that the close firm flesh about the knuckle, is by many reckoned the best, which is not the case in a leg of mutton,

A Shoulder of Pork is never cut or sent to table as such, but the shank-bone, with some little meat annexed, is often served up boiled, and called a spring, and is very good eating.

Edge-bone of Beef.

As this work is not a critical investigation of words, but relates merely to the art of carving, I shall not give my reasons for calling it an edge-bone, in preference to isch-bone, which is, in fact, the true name from ischium, Latin for the hip-bone, the former being that by which it is generally known. The following is a representation of it, and it is a favourite joint at table.

In carving it, as the outside suffers in its flavour, from the water in which it is boiled, the dish should be turned towards the carver, as it is here represented; and a thick slice should be first cut off, the whole length of the joint, beginning at *a*, and cutting it all the way even and through the whole surface, from *a* to *b*.

The soft fat, that resembles marrow, lies on the back, below the letter *d*, and the firm fat is to be cut in thin horizontal slices at the point *c;* but as some persons prefer the soft fat and others the firm, each should be asked what he likes.

Edge-bone of Beef.

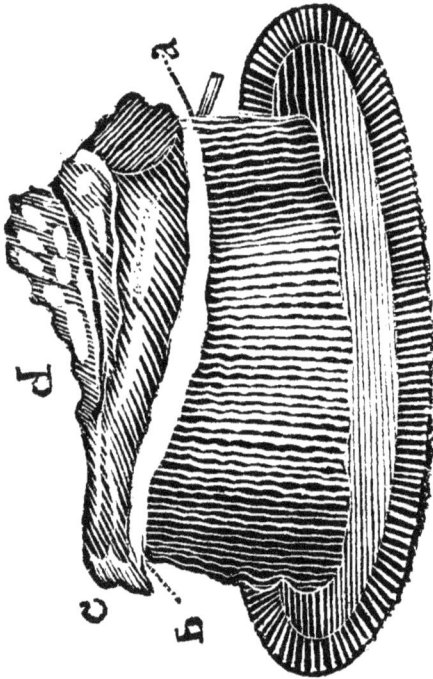

The upper part as here shown, is certainly the handsomest, fullest of gravy, most tender. and is encircled with fat; but there are still

some, who prefer a slice on the under side,
which is quite lean.   But as it is a heavy joint
and very troublesome to turn, that person cannot have much good manners who requests it.

The skewer that keeps the meat together
when boiling, is here shown at *a.* It should
be drawn out, before the dish is served up to
table; or if it be necessary to leave a skewer
in, that skewer should be a silver one.

A Saddle of Mutton.

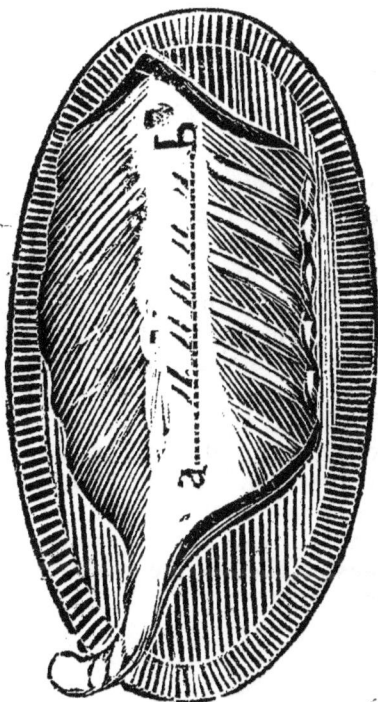

This is by some called a chine of mutton,

the saddle being the two necks, but as the two necks are now seldom sent to table together, they call the two loins a saddle.

A saddle of mutton is a genteel and handsome dish; it consists of the two loins together, the back bone running down the middle to the tail. Of course, when it is to be carved, you must cut a long slice in either of the fleshy parts, on the side of the back bone, in the direction *a, b.*

There is seldom any great length of the tail left on, but if it is sent up with the tail, many are fond of it, and it may readily be divided into several pieces, by cutting between the joints of the tail, which are about the distance of one inch apart.

A Breast of Veal, roasted.

This is the best end of a breast of veal, with the sweet-bread lying on it, and when carved, should be first cut down quite through, in the first line on the left, *d, c;* it should next be cut across, in the line *a, c,* from *c,* to the last *a,* on the left, quite through divides the gristles from the rib bones; this done, to those who like fat and gristle, the thick or gristly part should be cut into pieces as wanted, in the lines *a, b.* When a breast of veal is cut into pieces and stewed, these gristles are very tender, and eatable. To such persons as prefer a bone, a rib should be cut or separated from the rest, in the line *d, c,* and with a part of the breast, a slice of the sweet-bread, *e,* cut across the middle.

Breast of Veal, roasted.

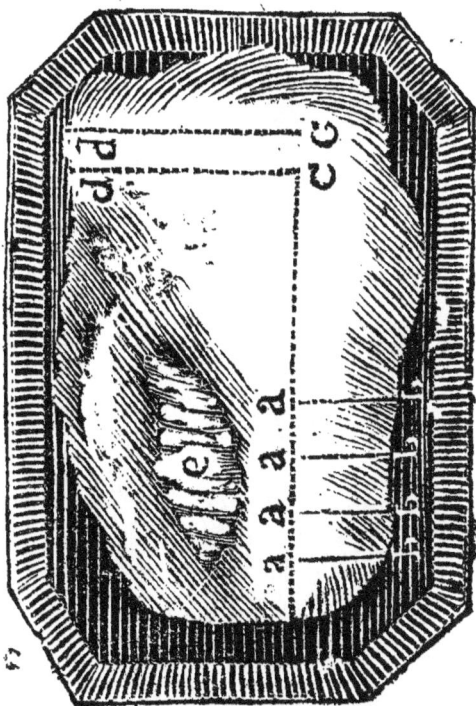

A Knuckle of Veal.

A knuckle of veal is always boiled, and is admired for the fat, sinewy tendons about the knuckle, which if boiled tender, are much esteemed. A lean knuckle is not worth the dressing.

You cannot cut a handsome slice, but in the direction *a, b.* The most delicate fat lies about the part *d,* and if cut in the line *d, c,* you will

L

divide two bones, between which lies plenty
of fine marrowy fat.

Knuckle of Veal.

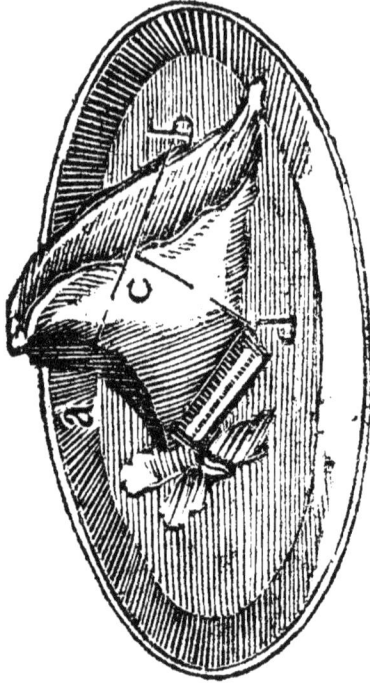

The several bones about the knuckle, may be
readily separated at the joints, and as they
are covered with tendons; a bone may be given
to those who like it.

A Spare-rib of Pork.

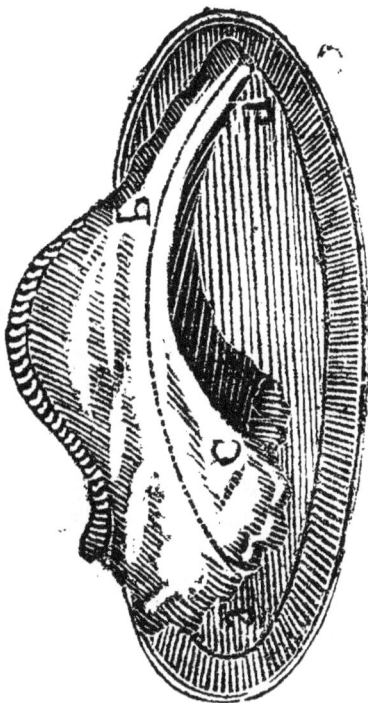

A spare-rib of pork is carved, by cutting out a slice from the fleshy part, in the line *a, b*. This joint will afford many good cuts in this direction, with as much fat as people like to eat of such strong meat. When the fleshy part is cut away, a bone may be easily separated from the next to it, in the line *d, b, e,* disjointing it at *c*.

Few pork eaters are fond of gravy, it being

too strong; on this account, it is eaten with apple-sauce.

Half a Calf's Head, boiled.

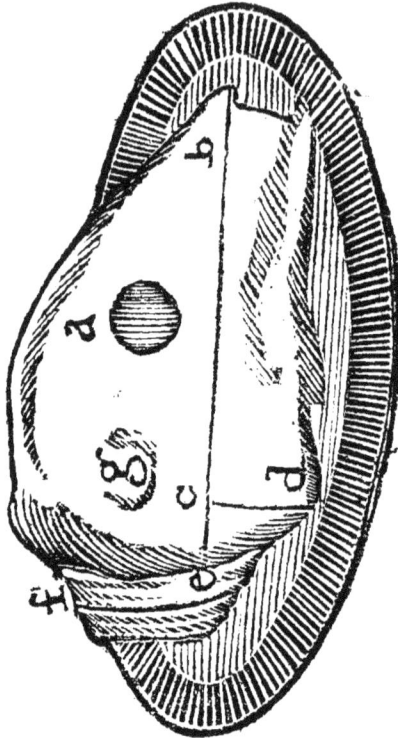

There are many delicate bits about a calf's head, and when young, perfectly white, fat, and well dressed, half a head is a genteel dish, if a small one.

When first cut, it should be quite along the cheek bone, in the fleshy part, in the direction *e*, *b*, where many handsome slices may be cut. In the fleshy part, at the end of the jaw bone, lies part of the throat sweet-bread, which may be cut into, in the line c, d, and which is esteemed the best part in the head. Many like the eye, which is to be cut from its socket a, by forcing the point of a carving knife down to the bottom on one edge of the socket, and cutting quite round, keeping the point of the knife slanting towards the middle, so as to separate the meat from the bone. This piece is seldom divided, but if you wish to oblige two persons with it, it may be cut into two parts. The palate is also reckoned by some a delicate morsel: this is found on the under side of the roof of the mouth; it is a crinkled, white thick skin, and may be easily separated from the bone by the knife, by lifting the head up with your left hand.

There is also some good meat to be met with on the under side, covering the under jaw, and some nice, gristly fat to be pared off about the ear, g.

There are scarce any bones here to be separated: but one may be cut off, at the neck, in the line f, e, but this is a coarse part.

There is a tooth in the upper jaw, the last tooth behind, which having several cells, and being full of jelly, is called the sweet tooth. Its delicacy is more in the name than any thing else. It is a double tooth, lies firm in its socket, at the further end, but if the calf was a young one, may readily be taken out with the point of a knife.

In serving your guest with a slice of head, you should inquire whether he would have any of the tongue or brains, which are generally served up in a separate dish, in which case, a slice from the thick part of the tongue, near the root, is best. Sometimes the brains are made up into small cakes, fried, and put round to ornament it; when so, give one of these cakes.

A Ham.

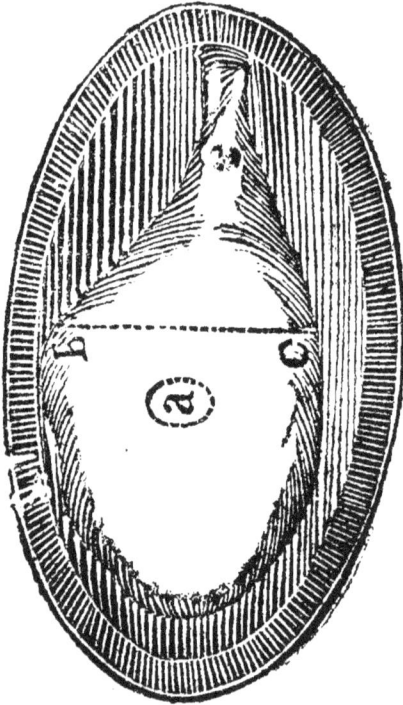

A ham is cut two ways, across in the line *b, c,* or, with the point of the carving knife, in the circular line in the middle, taking out a small piece as at *a*, and cutting thin slices in a circular direction, thus enlarging it by degrees. This last method of cutting it, is to preserve the gravy and keep it moist, which is thus prevented from running out.

A Haunch of Venison.

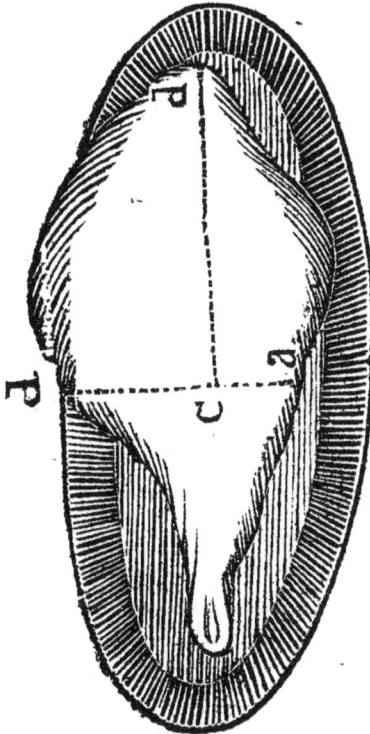

In carving a haunch of venison, first cut it across down to the bone, in the line *d*, *c*, *a*, then turn the dish with the end *a*, towards you, put in the point of the knife at *c*, and cut *

it down as deep as you can in the direction
s, b; thus cut, you may take out as many
slices as you please, on the right or left. As
the fat lies deeper on the left, between *b,* and
a, to those who are fond of fat, as most venison eaters are, the best flavoured and fattest
slices will be found on the left of the line *c, b,*
supposing the end *a,* turned towards you.
Slices of venison should not be cut thick, nor
too thin, and plenty of gravy should be given
with them; but as there is a particular sauce
made for this meat, with red wine and cur-
rant jelly, your guest should be asked if he
pleases to have any.

As the fat of venison is very apt to cool and
get hard and disagreeable to the palate, it
should always be served up on a water dish,
and if your company is large, and the joint is
a long time on the table, a lamp should be sent
for, and a few slices of fat and lean, with
some of the gravy, are presently heated over
it, either in a silver or a pewter plate. This
is always done at table, and the sight of the
lamp never fails to give pleasure to your company.

An Ox Tongue.

A tongue is to be cut across, in the line *a, b,*
and a slice taken from thence. The most tender and juicy slices will be about the middle,
or between the line *a, b,* and the root. Towards the tip, the meat is closer and dryer.
For the fat, and a kernel with that fat, cut off
a slice of the root on the right of the letter *b,*
at the bottom next the dish. A tongue is generally eaten with white meat, veal, chicken,

An Ox Tongue.

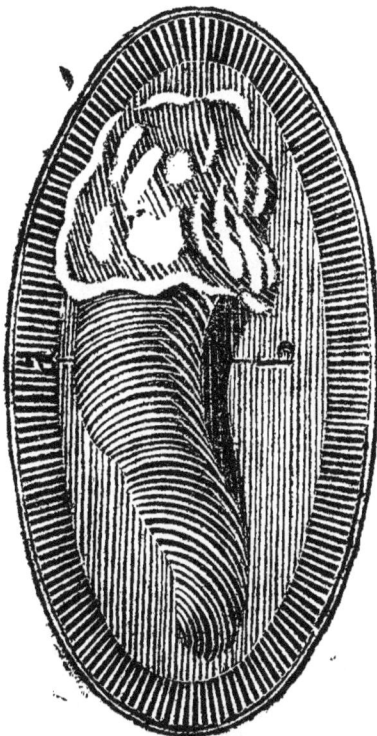

or turkey, and to those whom you serve with the latter, you should give of the former.

A piece of a Sirloin of Beef.

Whether the whole sirloin, or part of it only be sent to table, is immaterial, with respect to carving it. The figure here represents part of the joint only, the whole being too large for families in general. It is drawn as standing up in the dish, in order to show the inside or under part; but when sent to

L 2

table, it is always laid down, so as that the part described by the letter *c*, lies close on the dish. The part *c*, *d*, then lies uppermost, and the line *a*, *b*, underneath.

A piece of a Sirloin of Beef.

The meat on the upper side of the ribs, is firmer, and of a closer texture, than the fleshy part underneath, which is by far the most tender; of course some prefer one part, and some another.

To those who like the upper side, and rather would not have the first cut or outside slice, that outside slice should be first cut off, quite down to the bone, in the direction c, d. Plenty of soft, marrowy fat will be found underneath the ribs. If a person wishes to have a slice underneath, the joint must be turned up, by taking hold of the end of the ribs with the left hand, and raising it, until it is in the position as here represented. One slice or more may now be cut in the direction of the line a, b, passing the knife down to the bone. The slices, whether on the upper or under side, should be cut thin, but not too much so.

A Brisket of Beef.

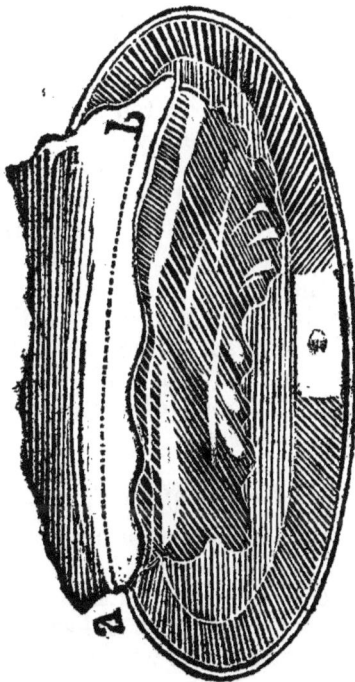

This is a part always boiled, and is to be cut in the direction a, b, quite down to the bone, but never help any one to the outside slice, which should be taken off pretty thick The fat cut with this slice is a firm gristly fat, but a softer fat will be found underneath, for those who prefer it.

A Buttock of Beef,

Is always boiled, and requires no print to point out how it should be carved. A thick slice should be cut off all round the buttock, that your friends may be helped to the juicy and prime part of it. This cut into, thin slices may be cut from the top; but as it is a dish that is frequently brought to the table cold, a second day, it should always be cut handsome and even. To those to whom a slice all round would be too much, a third of the round may be given, with a thin slice of fat. On one side there is a part whiter than ordinary, by some called the white muscle. A buttock is generally divided, and this white part sold separate as a delicacy, but it is by no means so, the meat being close and dry, whereas the darker coloured parts, though apparently of a coarser grain, are of a looser texture, more tender, fuller of gravy, and better flavoured; and men of distinguishing palates ever prefer them.

A Fillet of Veal,

Which is the thigh part, similar to a buttock of beef, is brought to table always in the same form, but roasted. The outside slice of the fillet, is by many thought a delicacy, as being most savoury; but it does not follow, that every one likes it; each person should therefore be asked, what part they prefer. If not the outside, cut off a thin slice, and the second cut will be white meat, but cut it even and close to the bone. A fillet of veal is generally stuffed under skirt or flap with a savoury pudding, called forced-meat. This is to be cut deep into, in a line with the surface of the fillet, and a thin slice taken out; this, with a little fat cut from the skirt, should be given to each person present.

A Fore Quarter of Lamb, roasted.

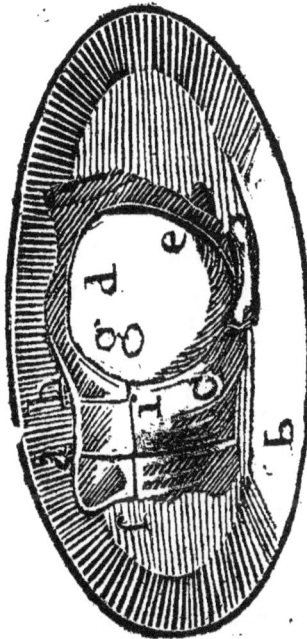

Before any one is helped to a part of this joint, the shoulder should be separated from the breast, or what is by some called the coast: by passing the knife under, in the direction c, g, d, e. The shoulder being thus removed, a lemon or orange should be squeezed upon the part, and then sprinkled with salt where the shoulder joined it, and the shoulder should be laid on it again. The gristly part should next be separated from the ribs, in the line f, d. It is now in readiness to be divided among the company. The ribs are generally most esteemed, and one or two may be separated from the rest, in the line a, b; or, to those who prefer the gristly part, a piece or two, or more, may be cut off in the lines h, i, &c. Though all parts of young lamb are nice, the shoulder of a fore quarter is the least thought of; it is not so rich.

If the fore quarter is that of a grass lamb and large, the shoulder should be put into another dish when taken off; and it is carved, as a shoulder of mutton, which see.

A Roasted Pig.

A roasted pig is seldom sent to table whole; the head is cut off by the cook, and the body slit down the back and served up as here represented; and the dish garnished, with the chaps and ears.

Before any one is helped, the shoulder should be separated from the carcase, by passing the knife under it, in the circular direction: and the leg separated in the same manner, in the dotted lines c, d, e. The most delicate part in the whole pig, is the triangular piece of the neck, which may be cut off in the

A Roasted Pig.

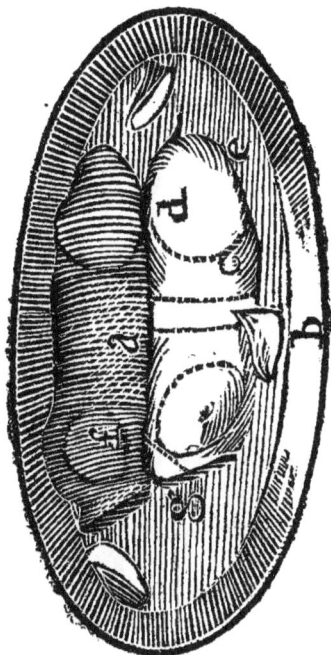

line f, g. The next best parts are the ribs, which may be divided by the line a, b, &c. Indeed the bones of a pig of three weeks old, are little else than gristle and may be easily cut through; next to these, are pieces cut from the leg and shoulder. Some are fond of an ear, and others of a chap, and those persons may readily be gratified.

A Hare.

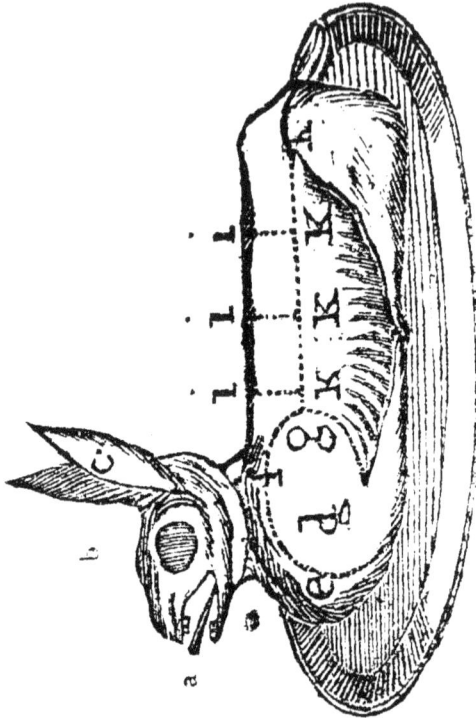

This is a hare as trussed and sent up to table. A skewer is run through the two shoulders, (or wings as some call them,) the point
of which is shown at *d*, another is passed
through the mouth at *a*, into the body, to keep
the head in its place; and two others, through
the roots of the ears, in the direction *b. f*, to
keep the ears erect. These skewers are seldom removed until the hare is cut up.

Now, there are two ways of cutting it up.

The genteelest, best, and readiest way, is to put in the point of the knife at g, and cut it through, all the way down to the rump, on the side of the back bone, in the line g, h. This done, cut it similarly on the other side, at an equal distance from the back bone. The body is thus divided into three. You have now an opportunity of cutting the back through the spine or back bone, into several small pieces, more or less, in the line i, k, the back being by far the tenderest part, fullest of gravy, and the greatest delicacy. With a part of the back should be given a spoonful of pudding, with which the belly is stuffed, below the letter k, and which is now easily to be got at. Having thus separated the legs from the back bone, they are easily cut from the belly. The legs are the next in estimation, but their meat is closer, firmer, and less juicy. The shoulders or wings are to be cut off in the circular dotted line e, f, g. The shoulders are generally bloody; but many like the blood, and of course, prefer the shoulder to the leg. In a large hare, a whole leg is too much to be given to any one person, at one time; it should therefore be divided, and the best part of the leg, is the fleshy part of the thigh h, which should be cut off.

Some like the head, brains and bloody part of the neck; before then you begin to dissect the head, cut off the ears at the roots, which if roasted crisp, many are fond of, and may be asked if they please to have one.

Now the head should be divided; for this purpose it should be taken on a clean plate, so as to be under your hand, and turning the nose to you, hold it steady with your fork, that it does not fly from under the knife; you are then to put the point of the knife into the skull between the ears, and by forcing it down as soon as it has made its way, you may easily divide the head into two, by cutting with some degree of strength quite down through to the nose. Half the head may be given to any person that likes it.

But this mode of cutting up a hare can only be done with ease, when the animal is young. If it be an old hare, the best method is, to put your knife pretty close to the back bone, and cut off one leg; but as the hip-bone will be in your way, the back of the hare must be turned towards you, and you must endeavour to hit the joint between the hip and thigh bone. When you have separated one, cut off the other, then cut out a long narrow slice or two on each side of the back bone, in the direction *g, h;* this done, divide the back bone, into two, three or more parts, passing your knife between the several joints of the back, which may readily be effected with a little attention and patience.

A Rabbit,

Is trussed like a hare, and cut up in the same way, only as being much smaller, after the legs are separated from the body, the back is divided into two or three parts, without dividing it from the belly, but cutting it in the line *g, h,* as in the hare; and, instead of dividing the head in two, a whole head is given to a person who likes it, the ears being removed, before the rabbit is served up. Many like the wing, i. e. the shoulder part.

A Goose,

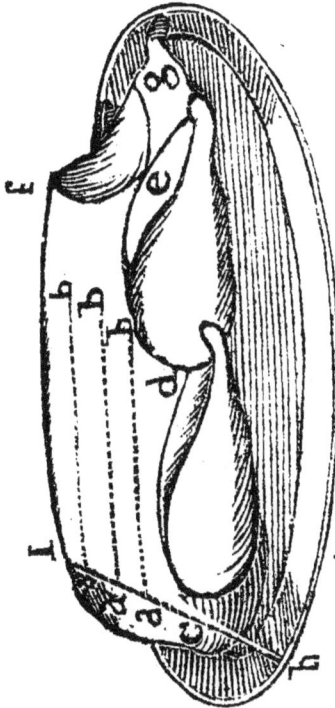

    Like a turkey, is seldom quite dissected, un-
less the company is large; but when it is, the
following is the method. Turn the neck towards you, and cut two or three long slices, on
each side the breast, in the lines *a*, *b*, quite to
the bone. Cut these slices from the bone,
which done, proceed to take off the leg, by turning the goose up on one side, putting the fork
through the small end of the leg bone, pressing it close to the body, which when the knife

is entered at d, raises the joint from the body. The knife is then to be passed under the leg in the direction d, e. If the leg hangs to the carcase at the joint c, turn it back with the fork, and it will readily separate if the goose is young; in old geese it will require some strength to separate it. When the leg is off, proceed to take off the wing, by passing the fork through the small end of the pinion, pressing it close to the body, and entering the knife at the notch e, and passing it under the wing, in the direction c, d. It is a nice thing to hit this notch c, as it is not so visible in the bird as in the figure. If the knife is put into the notch above it, you cut upon the neck bone, and not on the wing joint. A little practice will soon teach the difference; and if the goose is young, the trouble is not great, but very much otherwise, if the bird is an old one.

When the leg and wing on one side are taken off, take them off on the other side; cut off the apron in the line f, e, g, and then take off the merry-thought in the line i, h. The neck bones are next to be separated as in a fowl, and all other parts divided as there directed, to which I refer you.

The best parts of a goose are in the following order; the breast slices; the fleshy part of the wing, which may be divided from the pinion; the thigh bone, which may be easily divided in the joint from the leg bone, or drumstick, as it is called; the pinion, and next the side bones. To those who like sage and onion, draw it out with a spoon from the body, at the place where the apron is taken from, and mix it with the gravy, which should first be poured from the boat into the body of the goose, before any one is helped. The rump is a nice bit to those who like it. It is often peppered and salted, and sent down to be broiled, and is then called a devil, as I have mentioned in speaking of a turkey. Even the carcase of a goose, by some, is preferred to other parts, as being more juicy and more savoury.

A Green Goose,

Is cut up in the same way, but the most delicate part is the breast and the gristle, at the lower part of it.

A Pheasant.

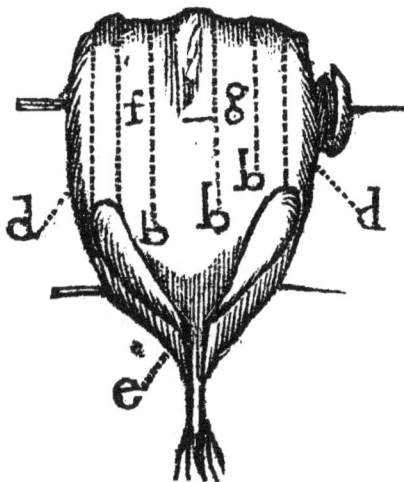

The pheasant as here represented, is skewered and trussed for the spit, with the head tucked under one of the wings, but when sent to table, the skewers are withdrawn.

In carving this bird, the fork should be fixed in the breast, in two dots there marked.

You have then the command of the fowl, and can turn it as you please; slice down the breast in the lines *a, b,* and then proceed to take off the leg on the outside, in the direction *d, c,* or in the circular dotted line, *b, d,* as see in the figure of the fowl, page 264. This done cut off the wing on the same side in the line *c, d,* in the figure above, and *a, h, b,* in the figure page 264, which is represented lying on one side with its back towards us. Having separated the leg and wing on one side, do the same on the other, and then cut off, or separate from the breast bone on each side of the breast, the parts you before sliced or cut down. In taking off the wing be attentive and cut it in the notch *a,* as seen in the print of the fowl; for if you cut too near the neck as at *g,* you will find the neck bone interfere. The wing is to be separated from the neck bone. Next cut off the merry-thought in the line *f, g,* by passing the knife under it towards the neck.— The remaining parts are to be cut up, as is described in the fowl, which see. Some persons like the head for the sake of the brains. A pheasant is seldom all cut up, but the several parts separated, as they are found to be wanted.

The best parts of a pheasant, are the white parts, first the breast, next the wings, and next the merry-thought; but if your company is large, in order to distribute the parts equally between them, give part of a leg with a slice of the breast, or a side bone with the merry-thought, or divide the wing in two, cutting off part of the white fleshy part from the pinion.

A Partridge.

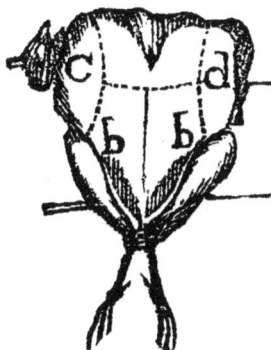

The partridge, like the pheasant, is here trussed for the spit; when served up, the skewers are withdrawn. It is cut up like a fowl, (which see) the wings taken off in the lines *a, b,* and the merry-thought in the line *c, d.* Of a partridge the prime parts are the white ones, *viz.* the wings, breast, merry-thought. The wing is thought the best, the tip being reckoned the most delicate morsel of the whole. If your company is large, and you have but a brace of birds, rather than give of-fence in distributing the several parts amongst them, the most polite method is to cut up the brace, agreeable to the directions given for cutting up a fowl; and sending a plate with the several parts round to your company, ac-cording to their rank or the respect you bear them. Their modesty then will lead them not to take the best parts, and he that is last served, will stand a chance to get the nicest bit: for a person will perhaps take a leg himself, who would be offended, if you sent him one.

A Fowl.

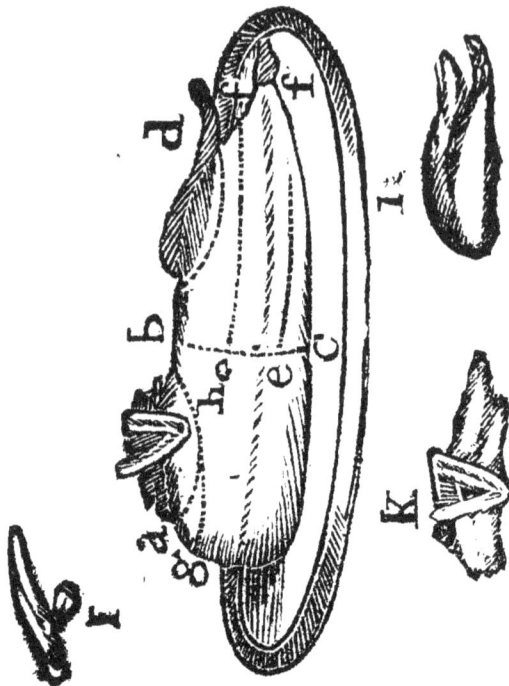

The fowl is here represented as lying on its side, with one of the legs, wing, and neck-bone taken off. It is cut up the same way whether it be roasted or boiled. A roasted fowl is sent to table, trussed like a pheasant, (which see) except that instead of the head being tucked under one of the wings, it is in a fowl, cut off before it is dressed. A boiled fowl is represented below, the leg bones of which are bent inwards and tucked in within the belly; but the skewers are withdrawn, prior to its being sent to table. In order to cut up a fowl, it is best to take it on your plate.

Having shown how to take off the legs, wings, and merry-thought, when speaking of the pheasant; it remains only to show how the other parts are divided; k, is the wing cut off, i, the leg. When the leg, wing, and merry-thought are removed, the next thing is to cut off the neck bones described at l. This is done by putting in the knife at g, and passing it under the long broad part of the bone in the line g, h, then lifting it up and breaking off the end of the shorter part of the bone which cleaves to the breast bone. All parts being thus separated from the carcase, divide the breast from the back, by cutting through the tender ribs on each side, from the neck quite down to the vent or tail. Then lay the back upwards on your plate, fix your fork under the rump, and laying the edge of your knife in the line, b, e, c, and pressing it down, lift up the tail or lower part of the back, and it will readily divide with the help of your knife in the line b, e, c. This done lay the croup or lower part of the back upwards in your plate, with the rump from you, and with your knife cut off the side bones, by forcing the knife through the rump bone, in the lines e, f, and the whole fowl is completely carved.

A Boiled Fowl.

Of a fowl, the prime parts are the wings, breast, and merry-thought, and next to these the neck bones and side bones; the legs are rather coarse: of a boiled fowl the legs are

M

A Boiled Fowl.

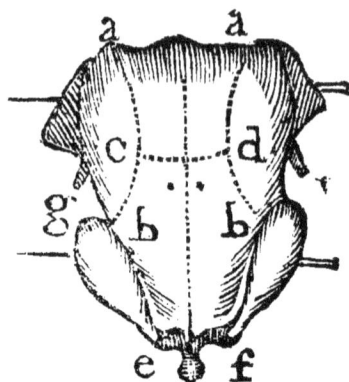

rather more tender, but of a chicken every
part is juicy and good, and next to the breast,
the legs are certainly the fullest of gravy and
the sweetest; and as the thigh bones are very
tender and easily broken with the teeth, the
gristles and marrow render them a delicacy.
Of the leg of a fowl the thigh is abundantly
the best, and when given to any one of your
company, it should be separated from the
drum-stick at the joint *i*, (see the cut, *viz.* a
fowl, page 264,) which is easily done, if the
knife is introduced underneath, in the hollow,
and the thigh bone turned back from the leg
bone.

A Turkey,

Roasted or boiled is trussed and sent up to
table like a fowl, and cut up in every respect
like a pheasant. The best parts are the white
ones, the breast, wings and neck bones. Merry
thought it has none; the neck is taken away,
and the hollow part under the breast stuffed

with forced meat, which is to be cut in thin slices in the direction from the rump to the neck, and a slice given with each piece of turkey. It is customary not to cut up more than the breast of this bird, and if any more is wanted to take off one of the wings.

Some epicures are very fond of the gizzard and rump, peppered well, salted and broiled, which they call a *devil*. When this is to be done, it is sliced a little way in the substance in several parts of it, with the knife, peppered and salted a little, and sent down to be broiled, and when brought up it is divided into parts and handed round to the company, as a *bonne bouche*.

A Pigeon.

No. 1. No. 2.

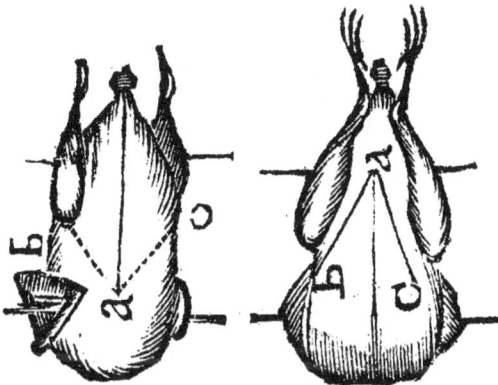

This is a representation of the back and breast of a pigeon. No. 1, the back; No. 2, the breast. It is sometimes cut up as a chicken, but as the croup or lower part with

the thigh is most preferred, and as a pigeon
is a small bird, and half a one not too much
to serve at once, it is seldom carved now,
otherwise than by fixing the fork at the point
a, entering the knife just before it, and dividing the pigeon into two, cutting away in
the lines *a*, *b*, and *a*, *c*, No. 1; at the same
time bringing the knife out at the back in the
direction *a*, *b*, and *a*, *c*, No. 2.

A Cod's Head.

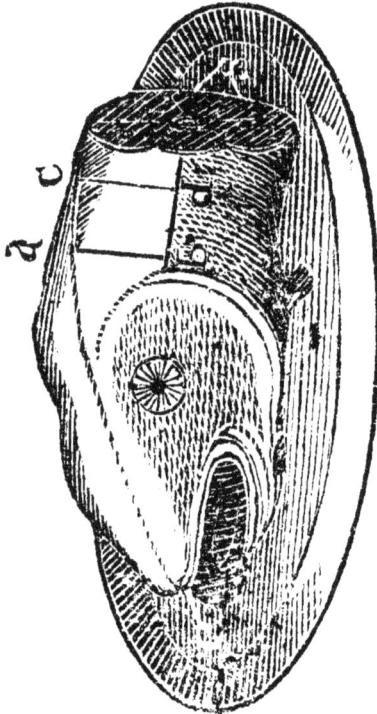

Fish in general requires very little carving
the middle or thickest part of the fish is generally esteemed the best, except in a carp, the

most delicate part of which is the palate. This is seldom however taken out, but the whole head is given to those who like it. The thin part about the tail of a fish is generally least esteemed.

A cod's head and shoulders, if large, and in season, is a very genteel and handsome dish, if nicely boiled. When cut it should be done with a spoon or fish-trowel; the parts about the back bone on the shoulders, are the most firm and best; take off a piece quite down to the bone in the direction *a, b, d, c,* putting in the spoon at *a, c,* and with each slice of fish give a piece of the sound, which lies underneath the back bone and lines it, the meat of which is thin and a little darker coloured than the body of the fish itself; this may be got by passing a knife or spoon underneath, in the direction, *d, s.*

There are a great many delicate parts about the head, some firm kernels, and a great deal of the jelly kind. The jelly parts lie about the jaw bone, the firm parts within the head, which must be broken into with a spoon. Some like the palate and some the tongue, which likewise may be got by putting the spoon into the mouth in the direction of the line *e, s.* The green jelly of the eye is never given to any one.

A piece of boiled Salmon.

Of boiled salmon there is one part more fat and rich than the other. The belly part is the fattest of the two, and it is customary to give to those that like both, a thin slice of each; for the one cut it out of the belly part in the direction *d, c,* the other out of the back in the line *a, b.* Those who are fond of salmon generally like the skin; of course, the slices are to be cut thin, skin and all.

A piece of boiled Salmon.

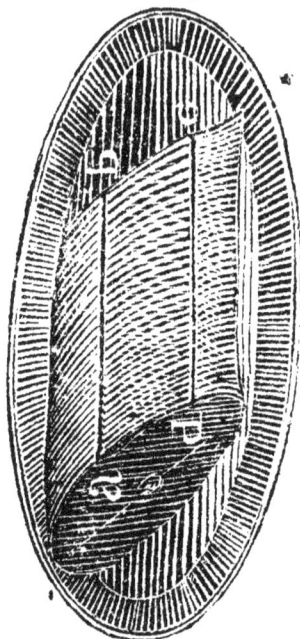

There are but few directions necessary for cutting up and serving fish. In *Turbot*, the fish knife or trowel is to be entered in the centre or middle over the back bone, and a piece of the fish as much as will lie on the trowel, to be taken off on one side close to the bones. The thickest part of the fish is always most esteemed, but not too near the head or tail; and when the meat on one side of the fish is removed close to the bones, the whole back bone is to be raised with the knife and fork, and the under side is then to be divided among the company. Turbot eaters esteem the fins a delicate part.

Soals are generally sent to table two ways, some fried, others boiled; these are to be cut right through the middle, bone and all, and a piece of the fish, perhaps a third or fourth part, according to its size, given to each. The same may be done with other fishes, cutting them across, as may be seen in the cut of the mackerel, below, *d, e, c, b.*

A Mackerel.

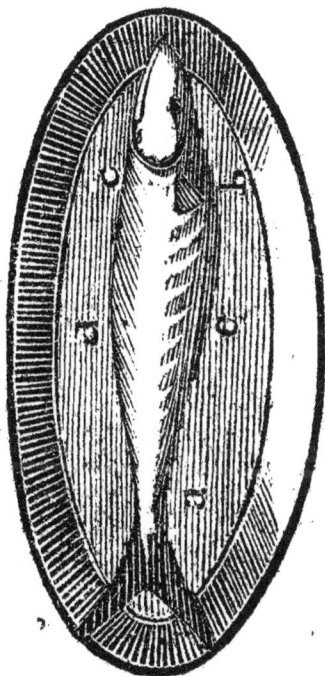

A mackerel is to be thus cut. Slit the fish all along the back with a knife in the line *a, e, b,* and take off one whole side as far as the line *b, c,* not too near the head, as the meat about the gills is generally black and ill-flavoured. The roe of a male fish is soft like the brain of a calf; the roe of the female fish is full of small eggs and hard. Some prefer one and some another, and part of such roe as your friend likes should be given to him.

The meat about the tail of all fish is generally thin and less esteemed, and few like the head of a fish, except it be that of a carp, the palate of which is esteemed the greatest delicacy of the whole.

Eels are cut into pieces through the bone, and the thickest part is reckoned the prime piece.

There is some art in dressing a *lobster,* but as this is seldom sent up to table whole, I will only say that the tail is reckoned the prime part, and next to this the claws.

There are many little directions that might be given to young people with respect to other articles brought to table; but as observation will be their best director, in matters simple in themselves, I shall not swell this work in pointing them out. Where there is any difficulty in carving I have endeavoured to remove it, and trust that the rules I have laid down will, with a little practice, make the reader a proficient in this art, which may be truly called a polite accomplishment.

THE END.

www.ingramcontent.com/pod-product-compliance
Lightning Source LLC
Chambersburg PA
CBHW032103280326
41933CB00009B/740